FLYING FREE

Also by Dan True

A FAMILY OF EAGLES

DAN TRUE

FLYING FREE

WYNWOOD™ Press
New York, New York

Library of Congress Cataloging-in-Publication Data

True, Dan, 1924–
  Flying Free / Dan True.
     p.   cm.
  Reprint. Originally published: New York : Dodd, Mead, c1984.
  ISBN 0-922068-12-4 : $8.95
  1. Golden eagle 2. Wildlife rescue. I. Title.
QL896.F32T783 1989
598'916—dc20   89-36810
                                                              CIP

ISBN 0-922066-12-4

Copyright © 1984, 1989 by Dan True
Published by WYNWOOD™ Press
New York, New York
Printed in the United States of America

•1•

Twelve eagle miles southeast of Amarillo the 16,000 acre Currie Ranch sprawls across Texas's panhandle. Half prairie and half mini-Grand Canyon, the Currie is a working ranch. However, the hundred-mile-long abyss gives the spread a ruggedness that makes it a natural for deer, coyote, turkey, bobcat, raccoon, fox, civet cat, and a variety of birds, including American and golden eagles. Rainfall in the canyon, called Palo Duro, is double the Grand's, therefore the eight-hundred-foot gorge is verdant: its floor is carpeted with buffalo, love, and gramma grass growing under cedar and juniper trees. Mesquite and cactus also dot the three-quarter-mile-wide chasm, while cottonwoods, willows, and cattails grow along the banks of a stream known as The Prairie Dog Town Fork of the Red River.

One March afternoon I hunkered inside a chicken wire photo blind a couple of hundred yards from an eagle nest. The blind was covered with burlap and cedar spray and built to the trunk of a cedar rooted on the edge of the Palo Duro's south rim. Scents of sage drifted from the prairie behind and mingled with the cedar's breath. My photo blind was near the middle of Currie

Ranch and I was poised to film action from a family of eagles.

Basically I was meteorologist for KFDA-TV in Amarillo, but in my off time I produced a weekly wildlife program called "True Nature." At my left shoulder stood a 16mm movie camera with telephoto lens. My lap held 8½ x 44 binoculars. The camera was focused on a mother-to-be golden eagle sitting on a six-foot-diameter nest built on a buff-colored rock ledge a couple of hundred yards upcanyon. The female eagle's primary color was milk chocolate brown, and she measured over three and a half feet, head to tail. Since February 22, twenty-one days ago, the hen eagle had pressed her brood patch, a spot on her breast which she can make bare, against two eggs. Twenty more days would bring the eggs to term. I find the patience nature programmed into female eagles remarkable. To sit for forty-one days and nights in one spot struck me as akin to being jailed. Across the canyon her mate sat on guard duty on Palo Duro's north wall. Palo Duro's walls were formed by rock layers of red, yellow, tan, and purple called "Spanish Skirts." The male eagle sat at the apex of a skirt, and with my naked eye his image looked as if a period had been typed on a cliff. I fine focused on the bird.

The male eagle was preening. Occasionally he glanced up and down the three-mile length of Palo Duro which the pair claimed as their territory. Suddenly he launched and headed upcanyon. The bird flew as if on a serious mission. I panned ahead of his flight, past a flat-topped bush marking the upper edge of his domain. A mile or so beyond the bush a white and black osprey, or fish eagle, was bopping along the rim toward the golden eagle's territorial boundary. I came back to the tercel. Racing along, he muted, as was his habit when purging his system for battle. I returned to the osprey. It was continuing down the rim. The two birds' courses would bring them together in less than a minute. I aimed and zoomed to the bush, focused, and zoomed wide to capture both birds. The gap between the tercel and the osprey was closing. Slowly I zoomed in at a rate matching their closure. They would be within fighting range in about thirty seconds. I glanced at the female eagle to see how she was reacting.

The hen eagle was following her mate's flight through eyes four times more acute than mine. As she watched, a wren flitted in and landed on her foot-thick aerie's fringe. The big bird raised her honey golden head and through amber eyes with black pupils she eyed the small one. I wished for two cameras. With apparent impatience the hen glanced between the wren and her moving mate. The wren hopped among the aerie's sticks, looking here and there. The eagle's head moved with the small bird. The wren grabbed a caterpillar and flitted in the direction of its nest in nearby rocks. The hen eagle stretched her neck and watched the little bird fly out of sight and returned her eyes to the male eagle. The golden eagle and the smaller fish eagle were almost upon each other. Expecting feathers to fly, I fine focused, placed my finger in position on the camera's release, and waited.

The tercel arrived over his territorial bush, faced into Palo Duro and rose on upslope wind that interfaced with the cliffs. The osprey came on. The male eagle had no way of knowing ospreys are fish-eating hawks with no interest in rabbits. To him the osprey was an intruder, and intruders had to be kept from the five to six hundred rabbits needed to feed the eagle's family in the coming year. When the osprey was a few yards from the bush marking the eagle's territory, the golden eagle dove at the interloper. In a flash of black over white wings, the smaller fish eagle turned on its back and thrust talons at the eagle. Golden wings blazed and eagle talons jabbed back. A white feather popped from the melee. The osprey righted and slid to one side, away from the eagle. Over his bush the tercel hung motionless, as though poised to attack again if necessary. The osprey eased away a few yards and hovered a long moment. Reluctantly the fish eagle turned away from the eagle's territory. The eagle watched, as if to make certain the osprey was no longer a threat. After the osprey was a good distance away, the male eagle leisurely cruised back and landed on his guard perch. He looked up and down the canyon, and preened.

Gradually the female eagle's inner set of eyelids, called nictitating membranes, closed. These opaque eye coverings are used by the eagle to protect her eyes when she catches and grapples with game in brush or grass. I shifted my camera to her and ran a few frames. The eagle's outer set of eyelids covered her nictitating membranes, and her head nodded lower and lower, until her beak touched the nest's sticks. I ran a few more feet of film. Friends often take oblique shots at my chasing birds and bees, and certainly home movies of an eagle's two sets of eyelids wasn't something I'd brag about. Most of the time wildlife photography is incredibly time

4

consuming, and sometimes I think I owe myself and people close to me better use of my gift of time. My friends remind me how nice it is on the golf course, the courts, and New Mexico's slopes. A swallowtail flitted in front of my blind, hovered a few seconds and went its way. I like courses, courts, and slopes. I also like wildlife photography. Sometimes I fantasize that through film, nature occasionally allows me to capture her soul. The female eagle's head jerked to attention and she eyed the canyon. After a moment her head gradually drooped again.

A haunting feeling tugs me to the eagle, a feeling that may stem from summers in the early fifties when, between college semesters, I flew a two-winged Stearman crop duster. I dumped tons of DDT onto Illinois corn and Mississippi and Texas cotton. Fellow pilots and I thought we were heroes saving America's crops and farms from enemy bugs. Then in the sixties, scientists found that DDT had a hundred-year life and was washing into streams and rivers and accumulating in fish. A short time later ornithologists discovered that when osprey and bald eagles ate DDT-laced fish, the chemical short-circuited many female birds' ability to metabolize calcium. As a result egg shells were thin and broke before hatching.

The tercel launched and flapped with determination again. I looked toward his territory's border. A red-tailed hawk was approaching. The male eagle easily repulsed the hawk and came back to his post. When he was settled, the hen eagle stirred in a way she did before either turning her eggs or leaving the nest to hunt.

The hen eagle slowly stood over her two eggs. Her

ova nestled in a soup bowl–sized, grass-lined nestcup, and each was over five times larger than a chicken egg. She looked at me suspiciously, I thought. The hen carefully curled her head under her breast. I started my camera. Gently the great bird turned a cream-colored egg, using her beak, chin, and throat. When she finished, she looked across the canyon, then turned her second egg. This one was also cream-colored but splotched with patches of rust. Golden eagles lay between one and five eggs but produce two two-thirds of the time. The mothering eagle cautiously lifted one foot outside the nestcup. Her legs were feathered down to yellow feet equipped with black, heavy talons with an inch-and-three-quarters curve. She withdrew her other foot and stood on the nest's sticks. Her talon spread was as wide as an average-sized woman's hand spread. Awkwardly, but gingerly, the eagle turned her body to the left a third of a circle. Her crop was flat, indicating she needed food. After standing a moment, she drew her feet into loose fists and carefully placed them one at a time on each side of her eggs. Then she slowly lowered her eight-and-one-half-pound body and rocked from side to side, positioning eggs, tarsi, and body exactly. The probable purpose of her one-third turn was to distribute her body's heat evenly to the eggs. She pulled a grass tuft from the nest with her beak and tucked it between the junction of her right wing and breast. Re-settled, the top of her body was flush with the nest's sticks, except for her head. I relaxed to await nature's next feature.

Archaeologists have evidence suggesting that Native Americans were watching Palo Duro Canyon's eagles twelve-thousand years before a group of Kiowa were "discovered" there by Coronado, when that explorer was making tracks across Spain's "new world." Nearing the canyon in April of 1541, the Spaniards were pummeled with thunderstorm winds and hail. After the storm the expedition's guide spotted campfire smoke curling from the canyon. Wet and tired, the hungry men worked their way over the rim and down into the abyss. On the canyon's floor Coronado found Kiowa Indians cooking buffalo meat under overhangs in front of sandstone caves. Following friendly exchanges the visitors broke out provisions and invited their Indian hosts to join them in a feast of thanksgiving. The Kiowa accepted, lit extra fires and contributed berries, corn, fish, rabbit, deer, and more buffalo. The festival ran two days and some historians look upon that party, seventy-nine years before Plymouth Rock's, as America's first Thanksgiving.

The lady eagle lofted her golden head and looked across Palo Duro. I sat up, lifted my binoculars and glassed across the canyon to the male eagle. All was well. I relaxed again.

Following Coronado's visit, the canyon became known as Palo Duro. Legend holds that the words are Kiowa for 'hard wood,' supposedly honoring the canyon's red cedar used for making arrows. However, since *palo duro* is also Spanish for hard wood, the natives may have borrowed these words from the explorers. Either way, after Coronado's visit the valley's aborigines lived undisturbed for three hundred years. Then, in 1846, treaty terms at the end of the Mexican-American war transferred land that included Palo Duro from Mexico to the United States. Following the treaty, U.S. Government hunters slaughtered southwestern buffalo in a strategy designed to starve the land's Indians out to make room for increasing numbers of New England's settlers. The buffalo's population was the greatest of any herd animal known on Earth; however, thirty years later, in 1874's summer, the animals were practically finished and the canyon's Indians had been reduced to rag-tag groups of holdouts. The groups were mustered by Chief Quanah Parker and the Indians fought on. After days of fighting, Colonel R. S. Mackenzie assembled his troops for an assault and charged the canyon. The skirmish lasted a day, and was the canyon Indians' last battle. Chief Parker and his followers were herded out of Palo Duro and marched a hundred and ninety miles to a reservation near Ft. Sill, Oklahoma. Soon after the Indians were gone, hands from the Atchison, Topeka & Santa Fe and the Fort Worth and Denver railroad gangs cut cedar from Palo Duro, milled the trees into ties, and laid rails into the Panhandle. When the tracks were finished, the Department of the Interior offered the "new lands" for twenty-five cents an acre. Newcomers flocked to where the railroads junctioned and a tent city flapped birth to Amarillo. Among the newcomers and land buyers was Jinks Currie, from Canada. Currie's purchase encompassed seven miles of Palo Duro. The sound of an aircraft drew my attention.

On the horizon across the canyon, a small airplane skimmed low over the prairie. I raised my binoculars. A red-and-yellow Super Cub was on the outer fringes of the eagle pair's territory, but over Currie land. Two persons were aboard. The airplane made a tight circle, resembling a maneuver flown by airborne coyote hunters. The aircraft dipped, and I heard the report of a gun. The craft circled twice and resumed course. I presumed the score was Super Cub one, coyotes zero. At the same time, I bet that the crew didn't have John or Hugh Currie's permission to aerial hunt the ranch. Recalling news accounts of eagles attacking aircraft, gliders, and helicopters I shifted to the tercel. He was in place, and I guessed he couldn't see the Cub because of rising ground behind him. I came back to the nest. The she-eagle was still. I shifted back to the Cub. The aircraft was cruising toward Owens Ranch and probably searching for more coyotes. Strange, the lengths some men go to prove they are macho. The aircraft droned out of sight. Its presence made me uneasy.

When I heard about the DDT and eagle egg connection, I went to the library for more eagle information. I discovered that the eagle, along with horned owls and vultures, is a living, prehistoric creature, with roots going back thirty-six million years, well before man. I wonder what went through their heads when they watched us two-legged, bare-skinned types mash our first footprints into earth's sands. And considering that the average time span of an earth species from emergence to extinction is estimated to be a hundred to five hundred thousand years, the birds must be doing something right. Isn't it possible we might learn something from eagles? Above the stream a red-headed woodpecker flashed into a cottonwood. I raised my binoculars.

The woodpecker had landed in front of its nesting hole. A black caterpillar was in its beak. The woodpecker poked half its body into the hole, as if feeding babies. It emerged with its beak empty and flew. A second later a starling landed at the hole, thrust its head in, came out with the worm, gobbled it and flew. I nearly laughed aloud and shifted my glasses in search of the woodpecker. On an adjacent cottonwood it was pecking and prying under loose bark. I hoped it was a good year for worms. Debating whether to shift my camera from the eagle to the red head's nest, I again wished for two cameras and elected to leave my one aimed at the eagle.

In the distance a Texas International 737 "diesel eagle" lifted from Amarillo International and banked for Dallas. A fly buzzed and landed on the back of my hand. I brushed the insect into flight. The jet climbed, thundered over Palo Duro and rumbled out of hearing. When silence returned to the canyon, I wondered if there is truth to the theory that every sound made on Earth remains locked within our atmosphere. Is it possible the roars of Tyrannosaurus and Diplodocus are floating in Earth's air, waiting to be heard again? Wouldn't it be a coup if an imaginative high schooler devised equipment that would unlock dinosaur roars and other sounds millions of years old? The hen eagle stirred. I started my camera.

The eagle rose, stepped to the front of her nest and dove off. Undulating seven-foot wings, she headed across the canyon. On top of her brown wings, about halfway out, was a brush of golden tan. The tan matched the color of her head. Her tail was also brushed with tan. Across the canyon the tercel was in the air, apparently coming to the nest to take his turn on their eggs. Above the stream the two eagles passed.

The tercel turned and followed his mate. His color was the same as hers; however, his wings spanned only six feet, and he weighed only about six pounds. Since man first noticed eagles, we have wondered why nature designed female eagles larger than males. I too have pondered that and have a couple of theories.

In close formation the two eagles flapped on across the canyon. At the rim, the female landed a few feet in back of the canyon's edge. The male landed beside her. After a moment, the hen leaned forward and flattened her back. The tercel lifted into the air, hovered and gently landed on top of her. The female gathered her tail fan to one side, and, manipulating their wings for balance, the eagles mated. After fifteen or twenty seconds the tercel lifted, slipped to one side and landed next to her. The hen roused her feathers, resettled, and awkwardly scratched her head with a claw. The tercel nibbled his beak through her head feathers, occasionally flipping away a tick or louse which had transferred to her when she had fed on a rabbit or other game. Each eagle was capable of grooming body parasites below its own neck with its beak, but neck and head critters must be eliminated by a partner. Multiplying parasites on an eagle without a grooming partner suck enough blood from ears and eyes to make the avian weak. Within weeks these head parasites can make the eagle too weak to fly, and starvation and death follow. I call the mutual grooming necessity "forced dependency" because it forces eagles to pair-bond. In man's cave-dwelling era, is it possible that man-woman dependency arose from differences in male-female size and strength? Were humans created with a size and strength

11

difference to force us to pair? After all, if we had been equally sized with equal strength, a cavewoman would have had no need for a man to provide game as large as deer and buffalo. Had we been equally sized, women would have been equally powerful as hunters. Under those terms, mightn't disputes between men and women over hunting grounds have disrupted establishing families? Since today's woman is more nearly equal in today's hunting grounds, America's corporate corridors, are male-female job competitions a factor in weakening family formations and increasing divorce rates? The tercel finished grooming his mate's head. The female eagle shook her feathers into place, turned to him and groomed lice and ticks from his head. When she was through, both eagles spread their wings and lifted.

In formation the birds rose to about three hundred feet. There the male backed his wings, sailed across the canyon, landed on the nest and belly flopped toward the eggs. His body only half covered them. The tercel raised himself, scooched over the nestcup and reflopped. His tail feathers stuck in the air, wing primaries angled up like a lady's hat plume, and his head aimed at the rock wall forming the back of the aerie. He had no bare brood patch, therefore he was more egg protector than warmer. Across the canyon, the hen rose on the wind and wheeled as she did when hunting. The Cub's sound intruded again. I turned to its direction.

The red and yellow aircraft was skimming a hundred feet or so above the rim, flying in the female eagle's direction. She held her position, as if watching. Then, tentatively, she turned away from the approaching craft. The airplane banked with her. The eagle tightened her turn. The aircraft's turn tightened. The eagle climbed. The Cub climbed. She turned more. The airplane turned more. A second later the roaring craft was beside her. Clamshell doors on the Cub opened. The eagle rowed her wings, started to climb, then hesitated, as though trying to decide whether to climb or dive. The rear passenger raised a gun, aimed at her and fired.

•2•

The female eagle thrashed, tumbled and pinwheeled down. Her body hit, bounced and congealed near the rim's edge. The Cub circled and lazily turned upcanyon. Arms shaking, I tried to read the plane's tail numbers. Images were too jumpy. I studied the pilot and his gunner for hair color, dress, or memorable features. Shadowy, shrinking figures in a shrinking craft were all I saw. My heart pounded, and I wished for a rocket launcher with an infrared-tipped missile that would home in on Cub engine heat. I returned to the female eagle. A breath of wind lifted the feathers of one wing and let it drop. Saddened, I lowered my binoculars.

Blasting an innocent creature into oblivion struck me as a poor demonstration of machismo. I groped for a reason and decided the men in the Cub probably had manhood problems. "Real men don't kill eagles," I whispered. When the Cub was gone I found limited solace in remembering that eventually bullies are thrashed, connivers outfoxed, and cheaters caught. Life is a circle. What goes around comes around. True, the coming around is often slow, and time between deed and just deserts frustrating. With patience as my only arsenal I watched the Cub fade. Feeling diminished and empty, I turned to the tercel.

The male eagle seemed to be looking in the direction of his lifeless mate. Is a "dumb animal" capable of understanding? Last year a yellow shafted flicker flew into my sliding glass doors and died on my porch. Before I removed the body, I discovered a ladderback woodpecker lying with its head across the back of the lifeless flicker. When I told that to Government wildlife biologist Richard Grimm, he related seeing an eagle take a rabbit to a mate that lay injured on the prairie. And how do we explain dogs lingering near dead companions? The tercel gazed toward the limp female and I wondered how long he would guard unhatched eggs. When hunger drove him to hunt, would he return? What happened if he hunted an extra long time? How much cooling could the eggs endure before infant life within died? But since he had no brood patch, the chicks were doomed, regardless. A voice within me urged me to do something. But it's a federal offense to molest an eagle or its nest. As my selves argued I realized that chill creeping into the eggs would soon deliver developing eaglet embryos into the hands of death. But what could I do? I had to be showered, shaved and dressed to leave the ranch for KFDA by four thirty. My watch read two forty-five, and again my inner voice urged me to at least do something. Go get ropes. Take the eggs. Deciding to worry on the run about what to do with the eggs after I took them, I hurried toward my tan Volkswagen parked under a cedar in a finger draw a third of a mile back from the rim. Currie Headquarters was twenty minutes away.

With a rooster tail of dust billowing behind I had three ideas: take the eggs to a commercial hatchery in Amarillo; buy a small incubator warmed by a household bulb I'd seen in my science magazines, and hatch them myself; or find a setting chicken. One thing was sure. The eggs had to be somewhere else by nightfall. A quarter mile ahead prairie dogs in a town on each side of the road scurried toward their mounds.

A mile and a half south of home I slowed, downshifted, turned right onto a rocky single lane dirt road and downshifted again. Within a short distance the trail dropped through a bumpy cut in the rim and descended along the spine of a grassy, cedar-sprigged ridge. A cottontail scampered into the brush. Half a mile later, down on my left there was a waterfall in a breathtaking setting I consider to be one of Texas's prettiest. During the twenties, thirties, and forties important visitors to the Panhandle were often brought to the waterfall area. It is a showpiece created by the relentless forces of time and weather. How nature formed this scene is worth telling.

Thousands of years ago storm runoff eroded a trench in the prairie. Subsequent storms deepened the trench into a draw, and eventually into a gulch. Additional runoff chiseled the gulch into a deep gash. At water-table depth a spring bled from the gash and became a liquid knife that cut deeper into the prairie. Eons of the spring's cutting plus seasonal rains deepened and widened the gash into a canyon. The canyon continued downward into the earth until it bottomed against a seven-foot-thick layer of bedrock. Here the developing canyon paused while its water, with help from storms, battered a hole through the rock. In time, water wore a hole in the rock, spurted through, washed earth from under the rock layer, and surged ahead. Under the bedrock, erosion tunneled a damp, dark hollow. Subsequent rains widened the hollow a hundred yards, deepened it to sixty feet, lengthened it an eighth of a mile, and opened wide its far end. One day the hollow's ceiling broke and crashed down. Instantly a steep-sided, boulder-strewn, horseshoe-shaped basin was formed. Spring water flowed over the edge of the original hole, tumbled sixty feet down, pooled, overflowed, and babbled among the boulders of the broken ceiling. Years later, willow and cottonwood garnished the stream's banks, ivy grew on the basin's walls, and grass grew between and around the boulders. The waterfall and its basin mark are Palo Duro Canyon's womb. On high ground back from the basin's east edge Jinks Currie had built his cabin.

Abeam of the waterfall I rolled up a shallow rise, leveled and passed between two windmills. The windmill on my left was an ancient, vine-covered wooden job that had probably been built by Jinks. A sparrow hawk watched me from the windmill's platform. The 'mill on my right was steel and provided water for headquarter's horse corral and stable. Ahead the north wall of Palo Duro Canyon loomed three hundred and sixty feet above the stream. The wall was a bowl-shaped curve matching a sharp right turn in the basin. Currie Headquarters nestled about two hundred yards from the bowl's curve on this side of the stream.

Headquarters was a four-bedroom main house of native stone, a one-bedroom stone bunkhouse-garage, a

17

blue tiled pool, and Jinks's original log cabin, made from cedar logs cut from the canyon. Cedar stockade fencing surrounded the houses, keeping John Currie's black Angus on their side of the land. Outside the fence, toward the canyon and stream, stood a fenced chicken lot. Two hundred yards in front of headquarters there was a small, falling-down place I call the "Hollywood House" because it was used in filming *The Sundowners* in the forties. In the Hollywood House's yard several wild turkeys raised their heads. Down in the canyon below my home was a nesting hen whose eggs were about to hatch. Turkey chicks had so far escaped my camera, and since the opportunity comes only once a year, I wanted to sandwich the filming of this turkey's chicks between eagle watching.

In front of the garage, I steered around a large mesquite and pulled onto a cement driveway. A red-and-white sign I had hung on the tree warned BEWARE THE DINOSAUR. When I opened my door, a red-shafted flicker flew from its nest in the mesquite's trunk and across the narrow canyon. As I walked to my house I decided to have a go at placing the eagle's eggs in a commercial hatchery.

Each hatchery I called said the same thing, "Illegal to hatch eagle eggs without a federal permit." One added, "Get a permit, we'll be glad to help."

Of course.

If I was to make KFDA on time I'd have to skip an incubator search, get the eggs and solve the problem of what to do with them on the run. I assembled climbing ropes, carabiners, Swiss seat and rope anchor webbings, a red nylon day pack to carry the eggs, aluminum foil to preserve what heat would remain of their mother's warmth, and a towel to cushion. Vaguely I banked on finding a setting hen, with a last-ditch option of pleading for one at the end of my six o'clock weather broadcast. Going out the door I had a new idea. If I replaced the eagle's eggs with other eggs, would the male continue to brood? If he fell for it, and I managed to get the eggs hatched, I could put the eaglets back in the nest for him to raise. I went to the refrigerator and got a couple of chicken eggs. Pleased with myself for thinking ahead, I hurried on.

On the cliff above the eagle aerie, I anchored my ropes to the trunk of a cedar, tied a Swiss seat on myself, attached a carabiner to the seat's front and, as mountain climbers say, "roped up." I put the pack on backward, over my chest, with the chicken eggs, foil, and towel inside. I took up slack and tossed rope over the cliff's edge. The tercel flew. I apologized to the bird, backed off Palo Duro Canyon's edge and rappelled down the cliff's face toward the shelf holding the nest. From the canyon floor a roadrunner clacked, and a scrub jay squawked.

Above the nest I stopped in midair. Suspended like a spider, I looked for the tercel. He was across the canyon circling. In his thirty-six million years on earth the golden eagle has never, until this century, had to defend its nest, because nothing but eagles could get to those high cliff sites. Although modern ropes have breached the bird's multimillennia innocence, apparently the eagle hasn't accumulated enough experience with man's nest intrusion to develop a defense. How many years would it take for the birds to catch on, I wondered, and let myself down.

Kneeling on the nest's sticks, I unzipped my pack, lifted the eagle eggs, wrapped them in foil, and put them in the towel. The eggs weren't warm. Moving as fast as I could I slipped them into my pack, placed the chicken eggs in the nestcup, backed off the eagle aerie and rappelled to the canyon's floor. When my feet hit ground I untied the Swiss seat and hiked a quarter of a mile along the canyon wall to a narrow, steep game trail leading up and out. Deer, Audad sheep, and coyote tracks marked the path. I climbed as fast as I could.

On the cliff above the eagle nest I pulled my ropes up and dragged them away from the rim. When I had them some distance, the tercel sailed toward his nest. Hoping he wasn't too surprised, I dropped the ropes to the ground and hurried to my car. At five after four, I shifted into high and roared ahead. On my right a coyote paused, turned sidewise, watched my approach a moment and broke into a run across the road. I wished I'd had time to see how the male eagle reacted to chicken eggs.

From my kitchen I dialed my neighbor Joe Detten to see if he had a setting hen. The first ring sounded. A year ago I bought a sick lamb from Joe to use in an experiment to test the myth about eagles killing lambs. The second ring sounded. I used a four-year-old-male eagle for the experiment. Third ring. Not only was the eagle incapable of killing the lamb, the bird was unable

to get talons or beak through the lamb's woolly skin.*
Joe answered.

Joe Detten didn't have a setting hen; however his wife
suggested I try the Don Glenns, a few miles down the
road toward Amarillo. I thanked her.

Billie Glenn said her son Mike had a red banty hen
that started setting yesterday. She would set twenty
more days. I told Billie I had a pair of semiorphaned
eagle eggs that needed twenty more days and asked if I
could bring them. She laughed, talked aside to her son
and said, "It's all right with us if it's all right with the
hen."

Skipping a shower I dressed in a suit and tie and
carried the eagle eggs to my car.

Past the windmills, the road curved right to match the
horseshoe basin's bend and descended toward the
stream. On my right the basin yawned. Approaching
The Prairie Dog Town Fork of the Red, I passed a
yellow and black sign I had erected that read CAUTION,
CROCODILE CROSSING. I splashed through the stream
a few yards above where it spilled off the bedrock's
lip and plunged sixty feet into the pool now popu-
lated by perch, a few catfish, and a couple of large-
mouth bass.

After fifty yards or so the trail straightened and ran
across rough rock paralleling the basin's edge, forcing
me to run in first gear. Creeping along I passed a black
and white sign someone else had erected that read
SPEED LIMIT 70. Ahead the canyon's wall rose. At the
wall's base the road left bedrock and became a steep,

*See *A Family of Eagles* by Dan True. Wynwood Press, 1989.

21

rocky switchback trail. Threading between car-sized boulders, juniper, squawbush, tamarack, mountain mahogany, scrub oak, yucca, and clumps of love grass the trail turned through five hairpins and rose up Palo Duro's north wall.

At the rim I passed through a cut, emerged on top, and accelerated along a cedar-dotted crown of land. On each side, jagged finger canyons emptied into the main chasm, and as I progressed the fingers shrank to gulches. With distance the cedar yielded to mesquite, and the gulches decreased to draws that blended into flat prairie carpeted with blue gramma and buffalo grass studded with yucca and mesquite. From Currie Headquarters to the gate serving the north side of the ranch it was four and a half miles.

At a cattle guard at the end of the ranch trail I unlocked the gate's chain, drove through and locked the gate behind me. My paper and mailbox stood outside the gate. I pulled onto Farm to Market Road 1151 without checking them and accelerated. A quarter mile down the highway I passed Joe Detten's house. Sheep and cattle grazed in his pastures.

In the Glenns' hen house Mike and I gently placed the eagle eggs in a nest box and under the warmth of a reddish banty hen. The hen had seven or eight eggs of her own, and by comparison, the eagle eggs were mountains. The hen resettled; however, the side of her with the eagle eggs tilted up. We laughed at her list, and I explained what had happened to the mother eagle. Billie said she was sorry, and that they had seen such an aircraft flying low across their land in the past. I was

22

about to leave when she asked about the male eagle. I told her about the chicken eggs, what I had planned and that if he were on the nest tomorrow morning we could rejoice.

Next morning the tercel was on his nest. He looked uncomfortable, but I was proud of him for being there. At the same time, I wondered how soon accumulating lice and ticks would force him to seek a new mate. When that happened would he leave the territory in search of a lone female with a parasite problem and an established domain? Feeling I'd done all I could, I crawled from my blind, coiled yesterday's ropes and left to have a go at filming turkey chicks.

Driving for home, I recalled my first attempt at filming turkey hatchlings. I was on Dewey Ashcroft's place, west of Amarillo. Rolling from under a cottonwood grove on a trail along a creek, a turn in the dirt road brought me face to face with a hen and her brood of about fifteen chicks. The little ones were tripping across short grass under their mom. I had eased my camera up, and although I hadn't seen turkey chicks in my viewfinder I was unconcerned, because finder images are limited. When my film came back from processing there were no chicks, only a mother hen. When I looked closely, there were small fuzzy blobs visible one second and gone the next. Rerunning the film showed the blobs were the little rascals flattening, burrowing under short grass and blending into invisibility. It was as if the earth had swallowed them up and was the best disappearing act I'd seen. The event had pushed my determination to expose wild turkey chicks to film. In front of the garage, I parked, took a 35mm camera from my pack and walked a rocky footpath down into the canyon, toward the turkey nest.

In the canyon just below headquarters, I passed an Indian cave in the sandstone cliff large enough to pocket a two-bedroom bungalow. As I walked between the stream and the mouth of the cave, I spotted the mother turkey and five or six chicks. Half stumbling, the hatchlings were crossing a layer of rock that was The Prairie Dog Town Fork of the Red's bank. I took three or four quick slides for insurance and moved ahead. The hen stepped along, clucking to her brood. One chick tried to burrow into a grass sprig growing from a dime-thin crack in the rock. The hen slowed. I hurried to get a close-up of the struggling chick. A few feet from the youngster I stopped and focused. Suddenly my viewfinder was full of mother turkey jump kicking at my camera like a karate fighter. To shield my face I held the camera at arm's length, pressed its shutter release and backed. She kicked my camera a good one and regrouped. From the way she glared and pranced there was no doubt that another attack was coming. Continuing to back and hold my camera at arm's length, I pressed its shutter again in hopes of at least getting a mad mother hen. The chick scurried to its mother. She turned and trucked down the stream's bank with her family. I don't know how long turkeys have tracked the Earth, but their dealings with man have obviously forced them to learn defense tactics. As the hen and chicks increased distance, I made plans to build a portable blind, set it at a scene of my choosing, get a sack of cracked corn and film turkey chicks on my own terms.

With the time I had left before going to work I drove around to the canyon's north rim to claim the female eagle's body. A limp cottontail lay next to her. I looked across the canyon to the male sitting on the nest and wondered.

Driving home with the eagle in my trunk I reminded myself that the fine for possessing an eagle, or parts thereof, was five thousand. To keep out of trouble I'd report my possession to Federal Game Agent Don Krieble in Lubbock. Don would pick up the female's carcass and forward it to the National Eagle Repository in Pocatello, Idaho. From there the eagle's feathers would be distributed to American Indian reservations where eagle parts are used in ancient tribal religious rites predating Columbus, Custer, and Colonel MacKenzie. This program enables Indians to use feathers that would have been wasted and saves the aborigines from having to kill an eagle for their rituals, which they may do legally under a grandfather clause. In my kitchen I gently wrapped the female eagle in a plastic bag and placed her remains in my freezer.

The next few days I spent much time keeping up with the tercel. When hawks or other eagles violated his territory, sometimes he flapped out and met the challenge, sometimes he simply sat and watched, as if torn between defending territory and protecting eggs. When he left to hunt he was gone between thirty and ninety minutes. Each time he fed, more fleas and ticks would transfer and eventually become a major problem. And while he was on the eggs he searched the sky a lot, as if expecting his mate's return. But that he was sticking with the chicken eggs gave me hope he would still be there when his eggs termed. Time would tell whether his eggs had been chilled beyond the endurance of life within them, or whether a banty had enough stuff to hatch golden eagle eggs.

•3•

For the Glenns' banty it was a struggle to turn eagle eggs, but she did it faithfully and as days passed, I came to regard her as a princess. With respects to Job, I'm surprised the adage isn't, "the patience of a brooding hen." On the other hand, the male eagle never turned his chicken eggs, but that was probably because without a brood patch he had no basis for understanding that necessity. I checked on him nearly every day, and one afternoon on my way to see how he was doing, I was nearing the prairie dog village when I spotted the eagle about three miles away. He was a speck rising on a light south drift on the other side of Palo Duro. Guessing he was hunting, I stopped to watch. While the speck in the distance climbed, I heard the prairie dogs bark. I shifted my glasses to the village.

Adult squirrels and youngsters stood on hind legs, looking my way. I beeped my VW's horn. The little ones disappeared below ground. The adults merely looked at me a short time and returned to grubbing for seeds and roots. They may have shrugged and said something like, "It's just that guy in the VW again." I shifted to the tercel. He was climbing out of about two thousand and apparently going for three. I shifted back to the village.

The young prairie dogs had popped from the ground and were facing me, standing like begging puppies and yipping. There was no doubt in my head about the eagle's knowing of the prairie dog village's existence, and I'd have bet that from his vantage point and with those eyes he was watching the little animals. As he climbed I wondered how much the youngsters knew about him. The distant speck continued rising, now toward the sun. I lowered my glasses, shaded the sun's disc with my hand and squinted at the male eagle. When he was about three thousand feet, I lost him in the sun's brilliance and returned to the prairie dogs. The adults continued foraging. The youngsters frolicked.

Three young prairie dogs played chase around a cone-shaped mound surrounding their dive hole. I pressed my camera to my eye, focused and filmed. While the tan, stubby-tailed youngsters played, an adult, I presumed was their parent, brought dirt up through the den's hole, mixed it with grass, molded it onto the cone's lip, urinated on the work, and with its paws tamped what would become sunbaked adobe. Increasing the cone's height probably came from an irrepressible instinct that drove the prairie dog to protect its den against flooding from future rains. The youngsters scrambled across the new mud and disappeared into the hole. The adult repaired damage and dropped behind the young. Facetiously I considered the wisdom of checking the critter's cone-building intensity before finalizing my daily forecasts. A second later the youngsters frolicked out again. I wondered where the male eagle was.

As I followed the little rascals' antics I was reminded

of speculation that when our forefathers came west, they probably called the frisky prairie creature "dog" because of its "bark." Biologically the animal is cousin to tree squirrels, but with no trees the squirrels were forced to live underground. Had the squirrel not barked, the pioneers might have taken the animal for food. Had that happened, the creatures might be protected today by a hunting season and enjoyed as game. The adult prairie squirrel surfaced with more dirt and worked it onto the cone. As it patted the uncured adobe I wondered about the possibility that Indians who used sunbaked adobe block for building may have learned the process from prairie dogs. Suddenly the whole village barked and scrambled into dive holes so rapidly they seemed to push and shove. A second after their short tails were gone, the eagle roared out of the sun and flew low across the village. Beyond the village's edge he banked toward the canyon and looked back over the top of his wing at the vacant village. Scoring it eagle zero, prairie dogs one, I speculated on what a great piece of film that event would have made. I drove on to my photo station near the eagle's nest. Thirty minutes after I was in place the tercel sailed in and plopped onto the chicken eggs. His crop bulged.

Watching a male eagle set a couple of chicken eggs day after day became as exciting as watching a haircut and promised dull wildlife film. Thursday afternoon was cloudy, nevertheless I got frames of the tercel rising from his eggs and scratching his head. Poor lighting because of the clouds rendered the film bland. It was all I had toward Saturday's program, due by five the following day, and I was about to allow myself a panic.

When it was time for me to leave I had some additional film so I searched for likely subjects on the way home. Past the prairie dog town I paused and filmed horned larks foraging on the prairie. Horned larks are the most common bird in the Panhandle, and I hoped program watchers would find that interesting. At the cut in the rim I got footage of a meadowlark singing from atop a mesquite. Progress, I assured myself and drove on. At the windmill I filmed a killdeer hobbling across the ground, giving its shrill call, circling with a wing dragging in the dirt and shuddering away in the direction he wanted to lead me. After I had footage of the bird's broken wing act, I searched for and found its neat cluster of four eggs. They were lying in rocks with their small ends toward the clutch's center. The eggs made good filming and I was encouraged about putting together a program I tentatively titled "Birds of the Prairie." I eased on. Nearing home a mocker flew into the top of a tree. I stopped and filmed again. When I finished, I considered adding a house finch, a few bluebirds, maybe a hummingbird, buzzards, and whatever else for a section on resident birds as compared to migratory birds of the Panhandle. Feeling confident, I moved on. As I turned into my driveway a five-foot diamondback rattlesnake lying on the cement filled my windshield. I stopped. The snake was apparently soaking up warmth left in the cement from yesterday's sun. "We've got a program," I breathed, then backed, parked and grabbed my camera.

From a respectable distance I set up, focused on the snake's head and rolled camera. The rattler's tongue flicked in and out. Since rattlers sunburn easily they are mostly night creatures, and I felt fortunate to be getting the film. As I filmed I recalled an old myth about cowboys circling their bedrolls on the ground at night with lariats in the belief that rattlesnakes won't cross a rope. It was a myth I had wanted to test. When I had all the film I needed of a rattlesnake flicking its tongue, I went for my climbing rope.

It would have been an unfair test to encircle the snake, so I laid rope in a line down the sandy driveway. Knowing it was a fifty-fifty chance that the snake would crawl toward my rope, I considered trying to herd the viper in its direction. I dismissed the idea as an incursion. From a distance far enough not to be intrusive, I waited. After about fifteen minutes the rattler slithered off the driveway, tracking toward the canyon, and angling toward my rope. I started my camera.

At the rope the snake turned and crawled along it. After twenty feet or so, the rattler crawled over the rope and on toward the canyon. As I watched the snake slither into grass, I was sorry the rattlesnake rope myth didn't hold. Even though I had proof that the myth was just that, if I were to bed down on the prairie I would still be inclined to circle my bedroll with a rope. Rewinding, I wondered, do we create myths as shields against threatening events over which we seem to have no control in order to soften dark realities? Anxious to share my film with "True Nature" watchers and happy to have enough film for Saturday, I dressed for work.

Friday noon in my den I was working on script to match my week's film when KFDA's assignment editor called. She said the National Weather Service had issued a tornado watch on a line of thunderstorms building across the eastern Panhandle. "We need you to film from the air any tornadoes that form." Unhappy at the interruption, I gathered my papers and a clipboard, pushed from my typewriter, changed from jeans to television dress and drove to the studio.

At one forty-five I sat buckled in the left seat of KFDA's parked 182RG munching a vending machine ham and cheese and working on the clipboard propped against the control yoke. The craft's wheels were on the grass edging the station's parking lot, and its doors were open against afternoon heat. Thirty miles east, the backside of thunderclouds formed a squall line running from Muleshoe to Pampa and into Oklahoma. Cameras lay on the passenger's seat. Beside them a scanner intermittently came on with police, sheriff, and highway patrol reports from under the storms. As I worked, a flock of sea gulls sailed across our strip, talking between themselves the way they do at sea. I paused to watch. Geologists have evidence showing that millions of years ago Texas and the Panhandle was awash with sea water from the Gulf of Mexico. Since these gulls were Panhandle residents, they may have descended from holdouts that preferred land to sea when the plains rose 3,500 feet and sent gulf waters to Houston. The gulls passed and I resumed writing. Before I finished a sentence a patrolman announced on the scanner's speaker, "Tornado on the ground two miles south of Claude." Claude is eleven minutes southeast and about sixteen miles north of Palo Duro. I hit the starter. Prop blast closed the plane's doors.

Nearing the black squall line at a hundred feet above Texas, I set my cameras for darkness expected under the clouds and reduced speed to prepare for turbulence. A moment later I passed under the cloud's edge and was over soaked cotton fields. Rain peppered the Cessna's windshield; however, the air was smooth. I peered ahead. No tornado. I bore on.

Half a mile under the cloud I flew into a wall of rain, and the aircraft bucked in turbulence born of shearing winds. Eagles probably have better sense than to fly in such stuff, and that could be part of the reason why they've made it through thirty-six million years.

After two or three minutes of being tossed between seat and belt, I was about to turn back when the patrolman's voice blurted from the scanner, "The tornado that was south of Claude has pulled into the cloud east of town." I could see our assignment editor frowning, dragging on her cigarette and blowing smoke. After a pause the patrolman said, "It stayed over open country. No damage." He probably had answered a dispatcher's question I was unable to hear. I could see our assignment editor mashing her cigarette. I turned for a course out of the cloud and descended to crop-dusting level. Ground effect dampened some of the air's roughness. I pictured an eagle hanging onto its perch or sitting on its nest in stormy weather. New rain beat the windshield. Sun was probably shining on the tercel's world. I calculated he was about eighteen miles and less than seven minutes away. I banked left and took a course in the direction of his nest. Cotton flashed below. Poison residue laid down years ago by fellow dusters was oozing toward The Prairie Dog Town Fork of the Red and Palo Duro Canyon. It's possible the eagle attracts me because I need to know if the bird's experience with

DDT is a bellwether for us. Odd, how both good and bad events from the past that appear innocent at the time cast bright beams or dark shadows touching so many.

In sunshine I looked back at the cloud. A double rainbow glowed against dark curtains hanging under its edge. I made a one-hundred-and-eighty-degree turn, framed the rainbows in my windshield, punched on the autopilot, filmed and turned again for the tercel's nest.

Within a few minutes I was approaching the thin line on the prairie marking Palo Duro Canyon's rims. Ahead, a herd of fifteen or twenty antelope with heads up stood on the prairie. The antelope looked like brown and white statues. I engaged the autopilot again and raised my camera to my eye. From behind the herd the buck pushed his harem and their offspring into a trot. As I drew near the herd broke into a gallop. Past the antelope I rewound. Then I connected the idea that buck deer and buck antelope keep their harems in front of them, for whatever that was worth. North rim passed below. In the air out over the canyon I descended a hundred feet below its rims, turned upcanyon and banked in and out of turns to match the canyon's twists. Below my wings the stream glistened. A quarter of a mile ahead was a dark spot on the cliff that was the eagle's nest. To slow the Cessna I reduced power, put its gear down and lowered twenty degrees of flaps. Nearing the nest I edged close to the cliff. The tercel's head was high and turned with me as I passed. "Hang in there, little buddy," I said, brought power and gear up, climbed out of the canyon and aimed for KFDA's tower twenty miles and seven and a half minutes away.

A moment later I passed within sight of Currie Head-quarters, Joe Detten, and the Glenns. The geography that gave birth to the waterfall and Palo Duro Canyon lay to the west.

During the next couple of weeks the male eagle continued brooding the chicken eggs, the Glenns' banty kept incubating eagle eggs, and the turkey chicks and I came to photographic terms. After "True Nature" with the rattlesnake and rope scene I got calls from a few souls irritated at my rocking their view of reality. The common complaint was that my test was no good because I hadn't used horsehair rope as had cowboys of the 1800s. I doubt if rattlesnakes care about whether a rope is nylon or horsehair. I didn't argue, but I wondered again if we create myths as substitutes for explanations of events that appear mysterious. My film apparently made few converts, and I mused at how easily we see only what we look for, or let set opinions prevail. But my curiosity had been satisfied, and that was the experiment's nugget.

March matured into April showers that greened the ranch's grass and germinated wild flowers on the prairie and in the canyon. The canyon's twenty or so American eagles left for wherever they spend the summer and black-chinned hummingbirds returned to the canyon from Mexico, along with black and turkey vultures, loggerhead shrikes, painted buntings, eastern phoebes, creepers, woodpeckers, redwinged and yellow-headed blackbirds, blue herons, cranes, a variety of shore birds, along with an assortment of butterflies and hundreds of hatching insects. Billie Glenn informed me weekly on the banty. Then, early Easter Sunday, she called and said, "Dan, one of our eagle eggs is cheeping." Excited as a prospective father, I drove up the cliff road.

Inside the Glenns' hen house with Mike and Billie, I watched Mike gently raise one side of the hen. Faint cheeps came from the cream-colored egg. We smiled and the hair rose on my nape. Carefully, Mike brought out the egg. The hen pecked at his hand and looked at Mike as if frowning. He handed me the egg. I felt uncomfortable. The eaglet inside cheeped again.

I studied the egg's shell. It was uncracked, and unpipped, and a new idea formed. Why not take the egg to the male eagle and let the eaglet come into the world in its own nest, with its father? Besides, it would be easier to deliver an egg back to the nest than a wriggly eaglet. I handed the egg back to Mike. "I'm putting this one back in its nest, this morning."

Mike frowned. "How long will it take?"

"If I rig my ropes ahead of time, forty minutes from banty to eagle."

He shook his head. "A chill could do it in, Mr. True."

I looked at Billie. "Do you have a hot water bottle?"

"No. Electric heating pad do?"

I shook my head and looked at Mike. "I'll wrap it in foil and a towel. The foil will reflect the egg's heat back into itself, and the towel will insulate and cushion."

Thoughtfully, he nodded. "Might work."

I headed for the door. Over my shoulder I said, "I'll rig my ropes and come back."

An hour and a half later, on the rim above the nest I tossed my ropes. As the male eagle flew across the canyon, I rappelled over the cliff's edge with the egg in my pack. My feet touched the nest. I kneeled and unwrapped the eagle egg. It was warm. I placed it in the nestcup. The eaglet inside cheeped. I glowed, removed one chicken egg, patted the eagle egg and whispered, "Your dad will be right with you."

From my photo blind I watched the aerie. Within a few minutes the tercel crossed the canyon and landed on his nest. On its front he stood still, as though listening. Then he turned and flew. He flapped with a determination that seemed to say, "I'm not sitting on that egg."

·4·

At one time or another you have probably experienced what is known as "buyer's remorse," those second thoughts after a big decision, such as the purchase of a high-money item. As the eagle rowed away I shook my head and said, "True, we should have left well enough alone." Across the canyon the eagle landed in the top of a cedar on the rim. The tercel clamped his beak on a sprig, cut the spray, and sailed back toward his nest. I bit my lip and realized then what an accomplished dummy I had been.

When the first egg begins cheeping the female doesn't leave the nest until the last egg hatches, which can be a period of time as long as three or four days. During these days the male eagle ceases performing the chore of "taking a turn" on their eggs. Since she has the family's brood patch, that makes sense. Throughout this time the male begins delivering green sprigs to the nest. It is an event eagle watchers don't totally understand.

The male arrived at his nest and placed the sprig in front of his eggs. Speculation among bird-watchers as to why the tercel brings a green sprig has been wide. Romantics say it is a bouquet the gallant tercel brings his lady. I appreciate the romantics' hope. However I have trouble believing gallantry among eagles would have utility. Other birders claim the bough's purpose is to increase the nest's humidity, but any increase would be infinitesimal. I have a third view.

In nature things and events generally have useful purposes. From that point of view, the sprig might be a fence to discourage baby chicks from venturing over the aerie's edge. I have never seen a sprig brought until just before hatch, and that makes me think the eaglet's first cheeps trigger a reaction within the male eagle commanding "fetch a fence." The tercel cocked his head to the egg, as though listening. A second later he turned, flew across the canyon again, and circled aloft into a hunting pattern. In a flash I realized that genetic codes were punching buttons in the eagle's head that impelled him to function as a father for the arriving baby eaglet, and suddenly I felt even more like a nitwit.

Almost without exception it is the male's habit to bring fresh game to the nest right after sprig delivery. Invariably that food is the first delivered to the aerie that season. Now, with or without a mate, the tercel's urge to bring protection and food for a youngster whose hatch was imminent apparently stirred fatherly instincts overpowering his sense of egg guarding. As he approached two thousand feet I thought it dangerous to let the egg chill more than another half hour. I sat down to wait and chided myself for not predicting his reactions.

Within fifteen minutes the eagle returned to the nest with a half-grown cottontail. He paused a moment, flew across the canyon to the cedar, broke another sprig and headed back with it. I hurried from my blind and rigged ropes to retrieve the unhatched egg and return it to the banty.

The egg was cooler than I expected. Quickly I wrapped it, placed it in my pack, rappelled down to the canyon floor and hiked to the rim. Driving across the prairie I realized that the last time I had heard the eaglet within the egg cheep was when I had placed it in the nest. I pressed my VW to its limit.

Cheeps never came from the egg again. The Glenns and I reviewed decisions I had made that led to the eaglet's death. I concluded that, after the fact, I had been negligent in not anticipating the male eagle's reaction to a cheeping egg, and that if eagles had courts I'd be found guilty of stupidity. How easy it is to verify a fixed past compared to predicting a fluid future. I was feeling lower and lower when Mike said that what we had learned could prove useful to other eagle watchers. I told him I appreciated his kindness, but wished I had waited and taken the eaglet alive to its father. Billie then pointed out that if a cheeping egg drove the tercel to bring a sprig, wouldn't a live, cheeping eaglet have driven him to react the same way? We decided probably so, and that the end result would likely have been a newly hatched eaglet left to chill. I shuddered and we agreed to let the banty hen hatch the second egg. "But who will care for the hatchling?" Billie wanted to know. I'd had enough problems for one day. Like Scarlett in *Gone With the Wind* I said I'd worry about that tomorrow.

A day and a half after we lost the first egg, Mike called and said the banty's own eggs were hatching and the second eagle egg was cheeping. When I got to the

Glenns' the banty was on her nest. A few of her chicks were on the hen house floor in front of her while another was popping from under her. One chick sat in the middle of her back. Mike slipped his hand under the hen and raised her. Only the eagle egg was unhatched. He let the banty down and asked, "Now what do we do?"

"Let's improvise an incubator. We can put the egg on cloth in a box, rig a bulb above it for heat and hatch it ourselves."

Mike and Billie grinned and Mike said, "Let's go for it."

Within a few minutes we had the egg nestled in a blue hand towel inside a tennis shoe box. While I rigged a sixty watt bulb above the nest, Mike called a hatchery and determined that between one hundred and one hundred and one degrees was the incubation for chicken eggs. Hoping eagles required the same temperature, we used Billie's cooking thermometer to control our incubator's heat by elevating or lowering the bulb. As we worked the egg cheeped. We smiled, crossed our fingers and waited. Forty minutes later a pip appeared in the egg's shell.

The egg rocked slightly as the eaglet inside positioned its feet and pushed the pointed node on its beak against the shell next to the original pip. In a moment another fracture broke a short line in the shell. For the next hour and a half the bird systematically turned and punched a line of connecting breaks around two-thirds of the egg's large end. Then, with a hard push against the bottom of the egg, the eaglet opened an egg shell door hinged by egg sac membrane across the unbroken segment of the connecting pips. The wet, struggling eaglet alternately rested and wriggled a few millimeters through the egg's opening. A few minutes later the baby bird pushed out of the shell that had been its home for forty-one days. We smiled, and Billie laughed and clapped her hands. "You've got an eagle chick to raise, Dan." My total baby bird experience was a half-naked sparrow that I fed bread and water when I was five. In one day the sparrow died. It takes nine weeks for a male eaglet to reach flying age, and eleven and a half for females. It also requires a hundred to a hundred and fifty rabbits. Happy as I was that the eaglet came into the world I wasn't anxious to become a full-time rabbit hunter. My joy at the eaglet's arrival suddenly dimmed, and I felt guilty for feeling that way.

The eaglet lay exhausted on the towel and gasped for air. Its eyes were closed, wet sprigs of down clung to its naked body, and its neck was curled in a sharp curve that put its head on its breast. I wanted to help straighten its neck, but since it had been bent so long I was afraid I might do damage. I frowned and looked back, as we're tempted to do when things go wrong and reminded myself that a month and a half ago when I decided to photograph the eagle family I hadn't counted on this. Uncomfortable at Billie's observation about having an eaglet to raise, I looked at the hen house floor, and to her. "Raising an eaglet is big problems."

"How so?"

"People-raised birds come to think of us as kith, kin, and parents. 'Imprinted' is what ornithologists call this bonding to humans. Animal behaviorists claim that such

42

birds transfer sexual responses to humans. They say imprinted birds are irreversibly impotent with their own kind, and impossible to straighten enough to qualify for life in the wild." I shrugged. "Raising this chick would be frustrating, a compassionate, dead-end road to nowhere."

Billie frowned and looked at the eaglet. "I'm sorry."

Over the next half hour, gradually, spasmodically, the little bird straightened its neck. As the chick dried, its down sprigs expanded a hundred times their wet size and covered its little form with a fluffy white suit. After resting a while the baby chick stirred, opened its eyes and tried to lift its head. A moment later it cheeped in tiny tones that obviously said, "I'm hungry, I'm hungry." Billie looked at me. "Fiddle faddle. I guess it's tomorrow, Dan." She laughed. "What do baby eagles eat?"

Feeling depressed and inadequate, I put Billie's question on hold. Then I remembered the law against having an eagle. I brightened. "It's illegal to have an eaglet. I'll have to call Federal Game and Fish Agent Don Krieble in Lubbock. Don will see that the bird is sent to a raptor rehabilitation center, where experts are experimenting with ways to avoid imprinting." I felt relieved. The eaglet cheeped louder. I glanced at Billie. "First food eagle mothers feed new chicks is usually rabbit lungs, then liver, and heart." The eaglet cheeped again.

Billie looked at the chick. "We're fresh out."

Although I had other things I wanted to do, it appeared I was forced into providing for a hungry eaglet. I frowned, snuggled the eaglet in the towel, thanked Billie and Mike, and carried the baby bird to my car.

From the seat beside me the eaglet cheeped. As I drove for home I pondered where I was going to get eaglet food, and how I was going to get it into its little system. I decided to call a vet for advice. I relaxed a notch and promised to call Krieble also, after I had the nestling settled and fed. I glanced at the eaglet and wondered if it was a boy, or girl.

At home I made a new nest of one of my T-shirts laid in the bottom of a small, corrugated box and put the eagle chick by a window in the den. The window faced the old, wooden, vine-covered windmill standing on a rise toward the waterfall. I rigged a bulb above the nest and laid my sling psychrometer next to the eaglet. The baby bird cheeped. I was tempted to answer, but decided that as long as I had it, I'd do my best to preserve the young eagle's wild identity of its wild self. I would not talk to the eaglet or look it in the eye. My job, I thought, was to give the bird loving care, but not let it know. "Call Krieble," a voice within prompted. "Soon as we feed the young one," I answered, and phoned a vet.

After I told the animal doctor my predicament, he asked, "Have a blender?"

"Yes."

"Feed the bird pureed rat or ground squirrel."

"Fur and all?"

"Fur is an excellent source of protein. Your blender will chop it enough to make it digestible."

I frowned. "How do I clean my blender?"

"Your problem."

I sensed he was about to hang up. "Wait a minute. How do I get pureed rat into . . . ?"

"Eyedropper." A dog barked in the background. "Good luck," he said and was gone.

The ranch had both ground squirrel and rats. I preferred squirrel in my blender, but reducing the rat population made more sense. Rats lived in a ranch dump a couple of miles away, up on south flat. I got my .22 rifle and went hunting.

After an hour and a half hunt, I approached home with a rat. I parked, walked by the pool, up the steps to my porch, and through sliding glass doors into the den. As soon as the eaglet saw me it flattened. I liked the bird's reaction.

Fifteen minutes later I knelt beside the nest box with a bowl of pureed rat. A little shaky, I opened the eaglet's beak and dribbled foamy, reddish gray soup into its mouth from the eyedropper. The little eaglet took the stuff. Proud of myself I sucked the eyedropper full and squirted more into its searching little mouth. The eaglet swallowed, gagged, coughed, thrashed, stopped breathing and quivered.

•5•

I grabbed the eaglet by its little legs, held it upside down and shook. The tiny bird coughed. Rat soup dribbled. I massaged the eaglet's chest. The bird snorted and gasped. It gasped again, opened its eyes and fluttered. I held it up to see its face. The eaglet's eyes were closed. After a few breaths the bird seemed better. In a moment it was breathing normally. I laid the baby back in its nest and whispered, "Little bird, out of respect to your mother, rest her soul, your father, the Glenns' banty hen, and a sixty watt bulb, please don't do that again."

The eaglet gaped, sneezed, lowered its head to the nest, blinked and looked as though nothing had happened. I reached for the bowl, sucked a small amount of puree into the eyedropper and was about to try again when my phone rang.

Al Hodge, pilot for Western Merchandisers was on the line telling me they had a new prop jet, he was leaving on a turn-around trip to Dallas in half an hour, and would I like to go? "Take us less than two hours round trip," he added with a touch of glee.

The eaglet cheeped. Al's invitation made me as frustrated as a hummingbird in a hurricane. When I told Al

46

I couldn't go, he paused long enough to allow me to explain. But how do you explain that you can't fly in a new prop jet because you have a sick baby eaglet, and make that believable? When we hung up I felt awkward. I took the eyedropper and cautiously tried again. The eaglet swallowed. I drew another portion of brew into the dropper, and put it into the eaglet's beak. Again it swallowed. I smiled. The eaglet cheeped and turned toward me. I fed it more, but its cheeping made me uncomfortable. When the eaglet had enough I stood and eased away. The bird snuggled down and soon was asleep. Its breathing was easy and so was mine.

After cleaning my blender with soap and water followed by alcohol, I phoned Krieble, told him how the mother eagle had died and that I had her body frozen. I also explained what had happened to the first egg. Don said he would love to get his hands on the pilot and gunner and was sorry we lost the first chick. "I'll pick up the eaglet and its mother's remains in a week or so." He added, "By the way, thanks for what you're doing."

When the rat soup was gone I spent two hours getting a cottontail in weather that was perfect for flying. I skinned the rabbit on an old room-sized cement pad a few yards downcanyon from the chicken lot. As I worked, a couple of prop jets droned by on descents into Amarillo International. Before I finished skinning the rabbit I picked up at least one flea I knew of. The critter sent shivers up my spine. Fleas were no doubt one reason wild eagle parents skin game that's to be fed to youngsters. Hurriedly I gutted the rabbit. Lungs, heart, and liver, I placed in a baggie. The minute I was through, I trotted to my house, stashed the rabbit meat in the refrigerator and dumped my clothes in the washer on the way to the shower.

Through the night the eaglet ate about every two hours. At a two A.M. feeding, I wondered if young eagles in the nest got midnight service. While I was carving a portion of bloody lung for the eaglet, the impatiently cheeping bird struck at a blood stain on the side of the box. Intrigued by its reaction I put a variety of colored marks on the box's inside. When the youngster struck only at the red mark I concluded eaglets come into the world with color vision and an inherited sense telling them "nourishment is red." A moment later, a coyote howled. It sounded as if the animal was right under the den window. Another coyote joined the first's howl, and another, and they had a yowling, squealing, yipping chorus. Since I moved to the ranch the little prairie wolves howled into my home often, prompting me to imagine they were complaining against Currie Headquarters house as a violation of ancient territorial grounds. From my desk I grabbed a tape recorder, recorded the coyotes' vocalizing, rewound, turned volume up, punched "play," held the machine to the screen and blasted the animals with their own voices. The critters hushed, and when they remained silent several minutes, I presumed they had packed it off. I chuckled at what the animals must have thought of coyote howls coming from inside headquarters.

At the end of a week the eaglet had grown at what I thought was an incredible rate. Curious about its weight gain in relation to food intake, I weighed the bird on gram scales at the beginning of each day. Next I weighed each day's total food. The little rascal was converting four ounces of rabbit into one ounce of eaglet growth. Currie Ranch calves needed nine pounds of feed to gain one. Human babies, I heard or read somewhere, require about twelve pounds of food to make a pound of growth. What powered the young eaglet's metabolism, I wondered, and mightn't the secret of its efficiency help human metabolism?

By week's end the eaglet started cheeping when I came in sight. Determined to keep imprinting to a minimum I didn't answer or look it in the eye. As a further measure against imprinting, when I fed the bird I wore a dark brown cotton glove that resembled a mother eagle head. To keep the bird from seeing I was attached to the glove I stayed out of sight below the box's rim.

The Monday morning after I'd been up feeding the bird for what seemed half the night, I was making up lost sleep when the phone rang. Krieble was on the line. My first thought was, he was ready to place the eaglet in a rehab center. My second thought was "Great, I can get my life back to normal." After good mornings, Krieble said, "First off, your eagle films are outstanding PR for the prey birds. We appreciate."

"Pleasure's mine." The eaglet cheeped.

"How's the eaglet?"

"Hungry most of the time." The bird cheeped louder.

A pencil or pen tapped in the background. "What have you heard about imprinting?"

"That it's supposed to be next to impossible to reverse."

The tapping stopped. "We'd like to test that theory . . . to see if an imprinted eagle can be returned to the wild, take a mate and raise young . . . the whole nine yards."

I yawned and wondered why that would be important when Krieble said, "We have two reasons for wanting to know. One, thousands of hawks, owls, and eagles that many of us in the office think should be released are being kept in zoos and by inactive falconers."

I have a thing about caged animals.

Krieble went on. "When we suggest that some of these birds be released, their keepers say, 'no, the birds are imprinted.' Off the record, I think that's an excuse, that a lot of these birds are kept as pets, and/or feather factories."

The eaglet cheeped again.

"An answer to this imprint thing could give us leverage to get some of these birds freed." He paused. "How would you like to be part of an experiment?" The tapping started again and stopped.

I sensed Krieble felt as I did about caged birds. "What kind of experiment?"

"We think it would be great if you'd raise the eagle."

I frowned and was suddenly awake. "How so?"

"To prove the imprinting myth either true or false for one thing. For another, if this DDT thing proves a long haul disaster, if a project like this works, we might offset that chemical misfortune by hatching and raising eagles, and releasing them to the wild." He paused again. "Didn't you crop dust?"

I hate explanations, and although I feel an obligation to the eagle, it takes five years for an eagle to reach sexual maturity. In an age of pressing problems such as the nuclear threat, improving my sand trap technique, and honing instrument flying skills, I had no business getting mixed up in a bird imprinting experiment. I was searching for something to say that would give me a respectable out when Krieble broke in. "We're reasonably sure if you raised and released the eaglet there it would never leave the ranch." He chuckled. "You don't plan moving?"

"We're" implied other people were involved. Why, I wondered, didn't he go for a sanctioned, funded, federal project? "I'll be here as many years as the Curries will let me."

"Good. Should be easy for you to keep up with her. This has the makings of a perfect test."

Five years? I wanted to ask and remembered that in Europe there is a record of an eagle that lived beyond a hundred. I frowned. "Why not send it to that center where they're experimenting with de-imprinting? Isn't that a government project? Trained people, the works?"

"Dan, as far as I'm concerned, we've got the best government in the world, but sometimes it works in strange ways. That project may take years."

I appreciated his impatience, but so could this one take years. Further, I dislike approaches to problems that take "the means justifies the end." Temptations to follow what appears to be a quick gain often turn into long losses. I wanted to suggest that we slow down and take time to get our official ducks in order. Krieble spoke again. "Besides, we think you're qualified. You took biology and animal behavior, right?"

Anthropology 125, "Man In Nature," came to mind followed by thoughts of animal behavior principles developed by B. F. Skinner and Konrad Lorenz. Visions also danced of an opportunity to shed light on the heredity versus environment controversy. Then "As the World Turns" popped into my head, followed by "but what an opportunity to photograph." Suddenly I was interested. "What do we do when I take vacations?"

"Fine. Keep records. And the more imprinting, the better. Talk to it, sing to it, dance with it. Really bend that eaglet's brain. We'll be in touch."

"Wait a minute." Again I wanted to ask about pursuing official permission and what happens when I vacation. Instead I chickened out and asked, "What about the legality of me having an eagle?"

"If the experiment proves out, we'll publish for the bird and animal behavior world. If it doesn't. . . ."

"Don, what about the legal thing?"

Pen or pencil taps. "I'll send a special permit application. Blanks will be filled in. Sign it and send it to our office in Albuquerque. We'll be in touch." He hung up.

With the phone in my hand I smiled and asked aloud, "Can a television meteorologist raise a semiorphaned eaglet in a little Texas canyon, and could the eaglet then overcome imprinting and find happiness back in the real world?" I cradled the phone. Then a dark cloud shadowed. "What if the bird got hooked on welfare and never attempted to go on its own?" I frowned, and wished I had asked Krieble if he had a plan 'B'. The eaglet cheeped.

•6•

I felt ambushed. If I were to invest time and energy into raising something, why not a child who needed adopting? The other side of me agreed with that, and pointed out how much wildlife photography and golf time I'd lose. "Doorstep child" and "instant family" floated through, along with concern of what the neighbors would whisper about a virile, intelligent, normal-appearing person raising an eagle, a bird a lot of people consider a lamb killer and child thief. As my two sides talked I reminded myself of the opportunity I was being handed to photographically record the life of a golden eagle. And if the imprint experiment developed new information on animal behavior, that cherry topping might offset the disadvantages. The eaglet cheeped. "I'll be there in a minute," I called. I fed it up front and didn't use the dark glove.

After two days of my talking to the eaglet it cheeped as soon as I came in sight. Falconers call such cheepers "screamers," and consider them bottom of the barrel birds. When the bird cheeped I always answered, and soon it learned to cheep at merely hearing me walk about the house. I also answered those cheeps, gave myself an A in Imprinting 101, and told the eaglet, "Little screamer, we're doing fine."

Within a week we *were* getting on fine as parent and child with occasional parent-child disagreements, particularly during nest T-shirt changing and wee small hour feedings. On the coin's other side, every four or five days I recorded the bird's growth on film. By May Day I had pictures of the eaglet making attempts at self-feeding. At this point I did a "True Nature" on the eaglet. Mail and phone calls indicated the program was warmly received. A baby bird, like a baby anything, apparently has universal appeal. Inwardly I smiled and looked toward the day when I could show film of a genuine eagle in flight.

As May progressed, night feeding ended. At the same time summer's warmth brought bass jumping in the waterfall pool, more prairie plants blossomed, range grass thickened, and mesquite put on leaves. Old timers in the Panhandle claim that spring frosts are over after the mesquite leafs. When I first heard the saying I humored the old timers. After several springs proved them correct, I swallowed what had been smug professional skepticism, and now Texas Panhandle mesquite and I are on good terms when it comes to the last spring frost prediction.

In late May, hummingbirds suspended a walnut-sized nest under a mulberry branch outside my bedroom door and laid two eggs the size of navy beans. A finch took up residence in the front yard and sang Spring's hope while a pair of eastern phoebes returned to nest on the back wall of the Indian cave. Ash-throated flycatchers also came back from their winter in Costa Rica and were catching flying insects along with scissor-tailed flycatchers from Mexico and Panama. Hundreds of cliff swallows reappeared and repaired mud nests across the canyon and caught an increasing population of mosquitoes. Mississippi kites returned from Central and South America to work on locusts, horned toads, snakes, and frogs. These falcon-shaped gray birds with three-foot wings and shrill whistles were such graceful flyers that I lost more time than I could afford watching them. By month's end the eagle had outgrown its box and where to put the bird had become a problem.

My garage was a possibility for a new home for the eaglet, but that would be a cage. The chicken house was a thought, but also a cage. The front porch was elevated and easy to clean by hosing down, and from it the eagle could fly whenever it wanted. I liked those features, and in the porch's corner I folded a green throw rug and put the eaglet in its new home.

During the fifth week, dark brown flight feathers covered the eaglet's downy underwear in a random pattern that made the youngster look scroungy. Around this time tiny deep blue pupils developed in the bird's ebony eyes and its voice deepened to a churp, reminding me that the father eagle's green sprig delivery ended at about the time a growing eaglet's cheeps deepened to a churp. I guessed a deepening voice signaled the parent bird that the youngster was old enough to decide for itself about dangers of the nest's edge. In the wild, it is also at about this stage that parent birds stop skinning their youngster's food. Glad to be free of that chore I, too, quit. However, feeding furred animals to the eaglet introduced the flea and tick problem. Fortunately nature has a way of minimizing parasitic accumulations on nestlings.

As provider for the eagle I had noticed that fleas and ticks vacate freshly killed game soon after death, as though leaving a sinking ship. Generally, by the time I skinned road-killed rabbits, most of their parasites had vamoosed. In the wild, I'm sure most fleas vacate rabbits by the time they are delivered to the nest. Nevertheless, as a precaution I dusted flea powder into the eaglet's head feathers every three or four days. Also, at this point in the eagle's life, I began to find fur pellets on the porch. These were capsules of fur mixed with bones that the eaglet couldn't digest. The pellets were about an inch in diameter and two and a half inches long. These "fur balls" swab out prey birds' crops, and when collected from under a nest or perch area, the balls can be analyzed to determine exactly what the eagles are feeding on.

One afternoon when I was watching the eaglet feed, a female Mississippi kite was sitting on a top branch of a front yard cedar. She had attracted the attention of two male kites that seemed to be trying to outdo each other in bringing her bigger and better insect gifts. I knew from past years' watching that the winner would gain the privilege of mating with the female. One at a time, a male landed next to the female with a bug in his beak. With what we would describe as tenderness the male offered the female his gift. She would turn her head, as people do to kiss, and take the insect. The female kite seemed to enjoy the attention and one of the males attempted to mate with her. The second male abandoned his search for insects, dove on his rival and raked its back with his claws. The mating male toppled from the female and was forced into flight, with the grace of a poolside spectator pushed into the water. Both males shrieked their shrill whistle as they circled and jockeyed for position to land next to the female. The males' rivalry became so lively I got cameras and filmed. At last one of the male kites won the female's favors and they flew off together, I suppose to build a nest and set up housekeeping and live happily ever after. She seemed to have chosen the male that provided the fattest, juiciest insects. I believe in the importance of love's power, but the female kite's reaction forced me to wonder how much weight human females give a man's status and/or earning potential when she chooses one from a field of suitors.

By the first week in June, the eaglet was the size of a goose and it was completely feathered. Its lengthening tail fan was marked with a broad white band and its legs were feathered to the ankle, making it look as though it wore brown pants. Feet were yellow with black talons that spread almost as wide as a woman's hand. The eagle's head was large, and that along with the size of its feet and overall size led me to believe the bird was a girl, so I named her "Lucy," after the character in the "Peanuts" comic strip. One morning, however, Lucy demonstrated she wasn't as sharp as Charlie Brown's Lucy yet.

I had gone to the porch to feed the eagle a cottontail when I found her missing. A hundred feet or so in front of the garage, a male Mississippi kite was buzzing a yucca. I went down the steps two at a time and trotted down the walk. The kite whistle-screamed, dove on a point near the yucca and pulled up. A small brown feather floated from the kite's wake. I hurried out to the yucca and found Lucy in the grass nearby. Blood oozed from a de-feathered, bald wound the size of a half dollar on the crown of her head. Her eyes seemed to say, "I'm scared to death." "Sorry, girl," I said. I admired her spunk at getting off the porch and into the world and took her move as a sign the call of the wild beat within her breast. I picked the eagle up. Her wings and legs thrashed, and she screamed in staccato. "Wait until you're bigger and older," I told her. For her own good, she'd have to be caged.

On the porch I put the eagle down and gave her the rabbit. She ate as though starved. I told her I'd attend to her head after I converted Currie Headquarters' chicken lot into an eagle aerie. I stepped to my garage and gathered weed-cutting tools.

Currie's chicken lot was a fenced rectangle thirty feet by fifteen. A wooden hen house with a slanting, corrugated tin roof faced into the lot and formed its west end. A locust tree grew inside the fence and about ten feet out from the hen house. After an hour's weed cutting, I carried Lucy to her new home. As we went into the lot kites circled above and whistled. Lucy kept her eyes on the birds, but they were unable to dive on her in the lot without crashing into the fence. When I put the young eagle down, she ran to a corner shaded by the hen house, turned her head to the kites and cowered. I told her I was on her side. The kites whistled. Lucy flattened and watched them. Sorry at how she was being treated on her first venture into the world, I went back to the porch and got her rabbit and carpet. When

I returned, a fly was sucking on her head wound. I brushed the insect away, lifted her from the ground and placed her on her pad. I was surprised when she flattened. "It's okay, Lucy baby," I said and left the rabbit. I stepped to the gate and outside. The eagle blinked. I latched the gate, went to my kitchen and called the vet for advice on eagle head wounds.

The vet wanted to know how she got a bloody head. After I told him he laughed, suggested that I smear the eaglet's wound with A&D ointment, and then get a shotgun after the kites. I thanked him for his medical advice, frowned at his solution to the problem, got a tube from my medicine cabinet and returned to the chicken lot.

Lice sucked at Lucy's wound. I was surprised at their number. She fought the ointment and I talked to her about that. With her head wound dressed, I took her by the ankles, laid her on her back and massaged flea powder under her wings and over her body. She fought that, too, and as I worked I recalled reading somewhere that three or four different types of lice live on birds. As I remembered it, there were body lice, front wing lice, rear wing lice, and head and neck critters. Each lice clan defends its territory of the bird against invasion by neighboring clans. Reminded me of a saying my biology professor recited as reflective of life, "Bigger bugs have little bugs upon their backs to bite 'em; little bugs have lesser bugs, and so on ad infinitum."

Next morning when I checked on Lucy, fuzzy growth, darker than surrounding plumage, covered what was bloody bare skin yesterday. Her recovery was so electric that I called the vet and shared the news. He said birds seem to have faster healing rates than most creatures. He volunteered that selective force may have evolved rapid healing in avians because birds must become airworthy soon after an injury, or starve. Broken bird bones, he said, knit to usable strength within a couple of weeks. He further explained that it seemed probable selective breeding favored birds that healed fast. The fast healers survived to breed while slow healers starved and fell by the wayside. He added that research on bird functions fostering fast healing might develop useful human applications. Made sense.

By the end of the seventh week, Lucy's new feathers completely covered her wound. The new growth was a bit off color, giving her crown a different look. Meanwhile, searching for and acquiring rabbits seven days a week, plus pressure to do my regular weather schedule and film "True Nature" kept me hopping. To make things more difficult, I had gotten most of the "easy" rabbits near home, and hunting was increasingly time consuming. Road-killed rabbits became valuable finds, and in a short time I was even peeling mashed rabbits from the road, thinking one flattened rabbit in hand was worth two plump rabbits in a bush. A pilot friend, Joe Mueller, called these pancake-flat animals "Sail 'ems," and claimed they could be flown like a Frisbee. I took his word for that. When I lifted these bloody messes, passing drivers stared. Driving to work one day, I calculated how many rabbits it would take to feed an experimental eagle five years. Fifteen hundred is what I kept getting. I shuddered and fervently hoped the imprint myth proved false.

By Lucy's ninth week she was fully feathered. When

she spent an increasing amount of time preening I presumed her genetic codes were instructing her to begin grooming feathers for a first flight. Her actions brightened my spirits and as a former flight instructor I began watching her development closely. One afternoon she was working the feathers of her right wing. Expertly she nibbled through one of her primaries, hooking barbs and vanes. As she worked a primary feather, it bent in a graceful curve filling me with aeronautical admiration. When she reached its end the feather snapped back. She roused, shook and stowed her wings. Tips of the longest primary in each wing met at her rump and crossed about an inch. Female eaglets I had watched fledge from canyon nests didn't make their first flight until primaries across rumps extended beyond the intersection three or four inches. Feathers of that length gave young girl eagles a span of seven and a half to seven and three-quarters feet, or six to nine inches more span than their mother's. In previous years I had also noticed that fledgling eagles develop an overall flight feather area about ten percent greater than their parents. After pondering the why of this phenomenon, I reasoned that the additional lifting surface would provide young birds with a lighter wing loading, permitting the youngsters to take off, fly and land more slowly. When learning to fly, slow liftoffs and landings would have obvious advantages. The larger size of the youngsters reduces top speed and zippiness. Then, at a year old when the young undergo first molt, Mother Nature would issue new, shorter feathers. Then the young eagle would equal her parents in size and zippiness. "Training feathers" is what I came to call this nest-grown set of feathers and as she worked them I thought of the importance of banding, or "ringing" her as the British say. I reminded myself to get a band from Krieble. Lucy was working another feather when my phone rang.

Don Krieble was on the line. "How's our eagle?"

"Imprinted and spoiled. She's a fine test bird. Have you an eagle band?"

"I have bad news." He paused. "The mayor of some town up in Iowa passed through Amarillo a while back and saw your program about the eagle from his motel."

I had depressing vibes and a sinking feeling and suddenly a band seemed unimportant.

"Seems the town's zoo lost their eagle to vandals with a bow and arrow. The mayor says they want your eagle."

I frowned and wondered why they couldn't get one from somewhere else.

"I told them to get one somewhere else, but within an hour, a call from the department in Washington said your eagle goes to Iowa."

It didn't seem reasonable. "Why would someone in Iowa be so determined to want an eagle from Texas when there are lots of others?"

"I wondered the same. But when I get a call from Washington, mine is not to question why."

Political influence reaching into the life of an eagle. What next? I wanted to ask Krieble if he reminded the politicians that we had nine weeks invested in this eagle, but remembered our experiment was unofficial so what else could we expect? A pencil or pen tapped in the background. "How soon do you think she might be ready to fly?"

"Week or so."

The tapping stopped. "My schedule won't allow me to be in Amarillo for a week, maybe longer." Krieble spoke with deliberation, as if he were saying more than he said. "Where you keeping the bird?"

"Chicken lot."

"Top enclosed?"

"No." I believed there was a message between the lines and started to go ahead and ask for a band.

"I'll call before I come."

I hung up, said aloud, "We're not beat yet" and dialed the vet. As soon as he answered I asked, "Is there a vitamin worth adding to the eagle's diet that will accelerate her development?"

"What's the hurry? It'll fly when it's ready."

Impatiently I blurted, "Could you just answer my question, please?"

He paused and I imagined he shrugged. "If it'll make you happy I have vitamins you can sprinkle on her food. But what's the hurry?"

I told him I'd be right there, hung up and marched down the walk toward my car. At the bunkhouse I had an inspiration on a way to help Lucy learn to fly sooner than normal. I went into the garage, got my chain saw, and headed toward a dead cedar a few yards beyond the chicken lot. Lucy churped at me. At the cedar I positioned the saw on a good-sized limb and pulled its starting cord. The engine caught and over my shoulder I said, "Little screamer, we're going to make eagle history. We're going to learn to fly a week early."

·7·

From the cedar, I cut a limb four inches in diameter and eight feet long and carried it into the lot. I aligned the log across the prevailing wind and wedged one end into a low crotch of the locust tree. Lucy waddled to her shady corner and watched me go and come. As long as she stayed curious I felt we had a chance to beat the odds. From the garage I carried a sawhorse into the chicken lot and placed it under the log's other end. Finished, I looked at the eagle and motioned to the suspended log. "Your flight training perch." I headed for my car and the vitamin run. Going away I glanced over my shoulder at the eagle. She was still lying in the shade. I wished for Dr. Doolittle's gift and vocabulary.

For the next three days Lucy continued to lie in the dirt, except when she ate. Discouraged, I ran through my inventory of myths about young eagles and their first flights. From childhood reading I recalled the story of a mother eagle that pushed her baby over the side, caught the youngster on her back, and piggybacked it aloft, followed by a another drop, and so on. As I recall the myth, the youngster soon caught on and flapped on its own. My young mind had felt for the fledgling. As an adult I had trouble with the myth because in physics

I had learned that Newton's Universal Law of Gravity has proved it virtually impossible for a mother eagle to push an eaglet over the side and then dive fast enough to catch a falling youngster before the baby crashes. Another myth claims parent eagles stop bringing food to the nest near fledge time. According to that myth the mother flies by the hungry youngster with a rabbit, supposedly to lure the fledgling into the air. I had trouble with that one because when I have watched young eagles leave the nest, parent birds have brought food a couple of hours before. Deep down I may have had troubles with both myths because I wasn't equipped to perform either. Then I realized that with a log perch, maybe I had a technical advantage over natural parents. To find out, I got a vitamin-sprinkled rabbit and carried it into the lot.

With the perch between Lucy and me, I held the rabbit for her to see and patted the log. "Up, Lucy." She churped, rose, waddled over and hopped on the perch by jumping and flapping. Not a lot of exercise for flying muscles, but as good or better than she would have gotten in her nest. I praised her as dog trainers do when an animal performs well. She kept churping, and before I had time to place the rabbit on her log she lunged for it. I dropped the rabbit and backpedaled. The eagle came off the perch to the rabbit, pounced and squeezed with her talons so hard she shook. Her aggression surprised me, but I took it as a sign that she had enough of a wild streak to overcome imprinting. At the same time her actions reminded me that when I first moved to the ranch I thought eagles killed by puncturing with their talons. I had pictured blood spurting from a rabbit through talon holes. Falconer Douglas Grayson taught me that prey birds kill by squeezing, like a boa constrictor. After Lucy squeezed a time that seemed instinctively determined, she relaxed, bent her head to the rabbit and fed. As she ate it occurred to me that I might encourage her to actually fly by placing the rabbit away from the perch after she had jumped up on it. As she ate, I told her, "Miss Eagle, we might give birth to new myths about how young eagles are taught to fly."

Next day I rounded the bunkhouse corner carrying another vitamin-laced rabbit by its hind legs. Lucy was on the log, facing into the wind. Balancing with her wings, she bobbed back and forth. On the underside of her flight panels about halfway out, at her carpal joint, there was a spot of white feathers three or four inches in diameter. These roundels marked her as immature and would be with her until she molted next year. Recognizing an opportunity to film an eagle learning to fly, I laid the rabbit down, dashed to headquarters house, got my movie camera and dashed back. With camera whirring I moved in for close-ups. As if on cue she bobbed and churped. A kite whistled from above. Unsteadily, Lucy eyed the bird and I said, "Look as if you were thinking about going up there and teaching those birds a thing or two, Lucy." She had a convincing look, until a swallowtail floated in front of her. Lucy's eyes locked on the butterfly and she twisted her head to follow its fluttering flight. At one point, she turned her head upside down as if to see the event from a different angle. With my camera running, I whispered, "Great." The butterfly flitted outside the fence and toward the canyon. I stopped filming but Lucy watched the insect until it was gone. I hoped she was tracking the butterfly for the practice she sensed she was going to need for tracking and catching game. Either way I treasured the film footage. I was rewinding my camera when my phone rang.

Larry Filkins, our chief announcer, was on the line saying a college girl classmate who was on the pro golf tour was in town and would I like to fill out a foursome this afternoon? How do you tell a friend, without coming off arrogant, that you don't have time to golf with a lady pro because you're teaching an eagle to fly? Can't you hear guffaws at that bit of gossip echoing amongst golfers in the clubhouse lounge?

When I returned, Lucy was composed. I got her rabbit and carried it past her. Churping, she ogled the rabbit while I took it a reasonable gliding distance from her perch. I placed the hare on the ground and stepped aside. With her eyes on the rabbit she moved her head side to side, like a belly dancer. I guessed her head movement somehow improved her distance measuring and I wondered if moving my head side to side would help me with distance gauging on approach shots. She raised her tail, leaned forward, muted, waggled, eyed the rabbit again, half opened her wings and shifted on her feet, as if to find a secure push off. Keeping her eyes on the rabbit, she moved her head side to side again, spread her wings, shoved off and sailed onto the animal. The fact that I had aided the young eagle with her first flying lesson gave me a rush, and for the first time I felt we had a chance at beating Iowa zoo folks and their darned political connections.

For the next few days when I fed Lucy, I placed her

rabbit progressively farther from her perch. As I stretched her aeronautical limits, her performance zoomed in spite of immature wing feathers. When she sailed from my log I took pride in the fact that our chicken lot practice was probably superior and less hazardous presolo training than her parents could have provided. (The year before, I watched an eagle pair invest almost six months brooding and raising a female eaglet that broke its neck on a head-over-heels first landing.) Although I felt good about Lucy's learning, with our days ticking by I remained concerned about progress in relation to the time we had to get her into the air. To increase the number of her practice flights, I began feeding her small portions of rabbit and making her fly three and four times a day.

A week after Don called, low gray clouds floated over the canyon on muggy air. On my way to feed Lucy a fourth of a sail 'em for breakfast, I stopped at the bunkhouse and peeked around its corner. The eagle was on her perch, facing the wind, and I allowed myself to feel a little smug. I couldn't tell how effective vitamins had been, but her primaries crossed her rump by about two inches. At that growth rate I estimated she'd be naturally ready in about a week. Tentatively, Lucy opened her wings. The breeze caught them. The eagle rocked, leaned forward and tightened her talons on the log. Gusts raised and lowered her wings. She turned her head and studied her moving flight panels. After a moment she looked straight ahead and leaned into the wind. Matching her body movements, I silently cheered her on. After a spell she relaxed and stowed her wings, crossing and recrossing their tips several times across her rump. She looked my way and churped. I withdrew. She hushed, sat a while and preened. Impatiently I glanced at my watch and adjusted it on my wrist. The eagle opened her wings, dropped to the ground, waddled to the corner and lay in the dirt. Disappointed and wanting her to try again as soon as possible, I gave her only half of the quartered rabbit and walked back to my house. On the way I realized that beyond Lucy's learning to fly, I had no ideas on how to teach her to catch a running rabbit, and that could be as important to deimprinting as her flight training. The thought unsettled me.

At mid-morning Lucy hopped on her perch. This time she was facing downwind. From my flying I knew her facing downwind wouldn't work. A second later she opened her wings about half their span. Negative lift resulting from wind at her back seemed to confuse her. She retracted her wings and I was astounded that she, of all birds, hadn't been born with knowledge of the critical effects of relative wind. She opened her wings again, and again she seemed confused. After a moment she turned on her perch and faced the wind. Her wings flew as they should and I thought I detected "Aha" going off in her head. I was sure she had learned the positive effects of facing upwind as opposed to the negative effects of facing downwind. I felt even better about Lucy's chicken lot training.

With the breeze flowing over her wings, Lucy opened and closed her fingers, manipulating her primary feathers and discovering new aeronautical secrets. With her wings spread, I noticed the tips of her fifth and sixth right wing feathers had two V-shaped notches about half an inch long where lice had chewed. I thought she was capable of managing these lice, but I promised to give her a dusting anyway. Lucy discovered that airflow through gaps in her tips gave her new control. (Aeronautical engineers call these wingtip gaps "slots" and design them into some aircraft to improve slow flight control.) While opening and closing her wingtips she also manipulated her thumb feather, the short feather fixed halfway down her wing's leading edge. This feather, called *alula*, meaning bastard wing in Latin, also functions as a slot. A gust knocked her off balance. She retracted her wings and stood still. Wind gusted again, and again, and after a moment she hopped to the ground, waddled to her corner and flopped. I got another fourth of the sail 'em and walked around the bunkhouse corner toward her.

As soon as Lucy saw me she got up, churping, jumped on her perch and stowed her wings. Her primaries had lengthened across her rump a fraction more than yesterday. She churped incessantly, causing me to think a reason falconers dislike screamers is because a screamer is a living advertisement that the bird was stolen as a chick and therefore as easy to train as taking candy from a baby. On the other hand, a silent falcon would prove it was caught wild, and its "manning" could only have been done by a hairy-chested macho man. At a gathering of falconers, it is probably socially superior to have a falcon whose silence attests to one's manhood. As I entered the lot, I told the screaming eagle about the importance of her practicing on that perch and what could happen to her if she didn't. As I placed the rabbit on the ground, she continued churping. This time I put it as far as the limits of the lot's fence would allow and stepped aside. "Go for it, Lucy." The eagle sailed off on a six-yard flight into the wind and softly alighted. Her flight was perfect. I told her she was a good bird. She "killed" the rabbit and tore into it.

Next morning was again cloudy and windy and when I found Lucy on her perch before breakfast, I felt as parents must when a child practices a musical instrument without being told. Along the leading edge of her wing from her shoulders out to her *alulae*, the eagle was opening a group of feathers forming a cuff. The cuff was hinged at its top along her wing. When deployed, it altered airflow in a way that increased her lift. (On jet aircraft, cuffs are made of panels called Kruger flaps that droop from the wings' leading edges.) With her cuffs deployed, a gust lifted Lucy off her perch. She retracted her cuffs and clawed for the log, at the same time popping up short scapular feathers on top of her wings. The popped-up scapulars had spoiled lift by wrinkling airflow. Cuffs and scapulars were operated by the eagle through a network of sinew under her skin. Since birds have no rudder, these "spoilers" when used on one wing at a time, provide control to induce banks for making turns. (Jet and sailplane wings have rectangular panels that pop up for turns and/or descents and after landing to increase weight on tires for better braking.) When Lucy dropped and grabbed her perch I smiled and hoped she realized she could fly, at least in a wind. I thought I heard my phone. I turned and listened. It was ringing.

Krieble was on the line saying that he was in town, that a representative of the zoo had flown in and was with him, and they'd be out within an hour. My heart sank, and as soon as we hung up I marched from the kitchen, out the door, and to the lot.

Lucy was still practicing. I walked up and unlatched her gate. The eagle paused and chirped. I swung the gate open, backed away and looked her in the eye. "Go." After a moment, she stopped churping, spread her wings and resumed practicing on her log. I wheeled, trotted to my VW and got a bloody rabbit that looked as if it had been hit by a Mack truck. As I approached Lucy looked at the rabbit and churped. I laid the animal in front of the gate. She turned on her perch, faced the gate, shifted her feet and moved her head side to side. Suddenly I realized that if she sailed through the gate she could damage her wings. I snatched the rabbit, held it behind me and backed away. Churping, Lucy tried to see the rabbit by looking around my body. I told her to wait right there and headed for the garage.

Among my tools I found a length of binder twine and tied it to the rabbit's leg. As I worked it occurred to me that if I fed her the whole rabbit, she might be too heavy, or contented, to fly. I got a pizza cutter, sliced the bunny in half and returned. Lucy was still facing the gate and churping. I went into the lot and placed the rabbit half on the ground almost under her. Stepping backward I played out twine. The eagle watched. Twenty feet from her I stopped. She studied the rabbit, moved her head, shifted her feet and dropped to the ground. Awkwardly she stepped to the rabbit, grabbed and "killed." I pulled the line. Lucy hung on to the rabbit with a vise grip, and as I pulled them along she balanced with her wings. Her hackles rose as I dragged rabbit and eagle through the gate.

When I had her a couple of yards outside, I stopped pulling. Lucy mantled her wing feathers, spreading and lowering them to the ground to hide the rabbit. She squeezed the flat rabbit with extra determination. A couple of minutes later she relaxed her mantle, bent her head down and studied the rabbit. She looked at me and mantled again. After a moment her hackles came down and she hooked her beak into what meat she could find and ripped. She'd feed about ten minutes. Krieble should arrive within half an hour.

As Lucy fed, I became concerned that maybe in my eagerness to see the eagle through our experiment I had read too much into the Federal Agent's phone conversation a week ago. He might have meant precisely what he said, instead of what I thought he said, and would be irritated at what I'd done. I told Lucy that my letting her out of her cage might aggravate a man named Don Krieble who was on his way to the ranch and expecting to cage her and take her to a town far away. I sat down near her on the ground. "We're going to be honest with Mr. K, Lucy." I shifted. "Honest as Mother Nature. If there are consequences, I'll take them." I glanced at her. She gulped a bite and eyed me, and I imagined she was agreeing. I leaned back and said, "Yes, sir, the way to avoid trouble in this life is to play it straight." She tore at the rabbit again. "If we'd done this experiment straight, we wouldn't be in trouble now." She gulped another bite. Above us a Mississippi kite whistled. We looked up. The kite clawed a locust

73

out of the air, turned and sailed in the direction of a tree that I suspected held its nest. With its beak the kite clipped the locust's wings and legs as it flew. The parts drifted down behind the kite. Lucy resumed feeding. "I admire the simplicity of your life, Lucy." She swallowed and tore another bite. I reminded her that when she was hungry she shouldn't depend on me, that with those wings and talons all she had to do was swing lazy circles in the cool blue sky until she spotted a rabbit. I reminded her that after she ate she wouldn't have dishes to do or garbage to wrap. I smiled and told her she was lucky. "No taxes, no insurance payments, no parking tickets, no inflation, or utility bills." We agreed that on the other hand she'd have a heck of a problem if she flew into a fence and broke a wing, or picked up a load of poison from a rat or rabbit meal. "And keep a sharp eye for trigger-happy hunters," I warned. We also covered the fact she might get hungry and cold while grounded two or three days by a howling blizzard. But when it came to teaching the kids, all they needed to know was how to catch rabbits. Two, maybe three days educating at the most. "With cheep tuition." I chuckled at my pun and suddenly realized I was talking to an eagle. I felt silly. I stood and told Lucy I was going to leave a note on the door telling Krieble where I was. "Excuse me," I said and left.

When I came back Lucy was inside the chicken lot and back on her perch. She churped, and I felt like laughing and crying. Then it occurred to me that the eagle's freedom lay in her head, that even with over seven-foot wings fitted with marvelous flight devices, she was caged by her mind. She reminded me of people

I'd known who shackled themselves by caging their capabilities.

Behind me, from the direction of the cut in the rim where the switchback begins, I heard the sound of a vehicle. A green pickup with a crate in its bed downshifted and turned into the first hairpin. I went into the chicken lot and shooed Lucy off her perch. She ran to her corner. Quickly I dismantled her perch, dragged it and the sawhorse out of the lot and reassembled them with one end of the log anchored into the fence. I herded Lucy out the gate. Reluctantly she waddled out and jump-flapped up to her perch. Above us a Mississippi kite whistled. She looked at the kite, roused and shook. I closed the gate. The truck reached the bottom of the trail and rolled onto bedrock. I scowled at the eagle. We're running out of time, Lucy.

The eagle preened.

·8·

Krieble's truck rolled on. Lucy continued preening. It was tempting to think that the eagle was experimenting with independence, like a teenager. But that would be anthropomorphic, possibly arrogant. Nevertheless, if she were experimenting, I wished she had chosen another time and place.

Don parked in front of my house. A trim brunette dressed in a white western-cut shirt, designer jeans, and tan cowboy boots was with him. Don opened the gate for her, headed up my walk and waved. I waved back. On the steps Don said, "Mrs. Allison, meet Dan True." He turned to me. "Mrs. Allison is the mayor's wife."

"Hi, Dan." She smiled with honesty. "I've heard a lot about your eagle. Pity about its mother."

She seemed like a nice lady, but I didn't like her being there. "Hi." I wanted to ask her why they were insistent on acquiring Lucy. Her brown eyes surveyed my home and the canyon. She drank it in and for a moment seemed far away. At last she said, "My grandfather worked here as a teenage cowboy." Don's eyes met mine and she added, "What a lovely place."

From somewhere a wren warbled. She looked around. "Where is the eagle?"

I swallowed. "Chicken lot."

From the lot's direction a mockingbird began its musical treasury. Mrs. Allison smiled. Don motioned to his truck and glanced at me. "Can we drive there?"

The mocker sang a new stanza. I nodded. "I'll . . ." I had to clear my throat. "I'll go with you." I felt like a kid on his way to the woodshed.

When we turned the garage's corner, Lucy was sitting on the front edge of the hen house's slanted tin roof, churping at us. Mrs. Allison leaned forward to the edge of her seat. "What's it doing there?"

Krieble braked to a stop and looked across Mrs. Allison at me. I was torn between saying, "How 'bout that? An eagle on a hot tin roof," and mustering courage to tell him I had let her out. Instead I shrugged. "Just getting a little exercise. She's too imprinted to fly."

Mrs. Allison touched my arm. "How sweet." Then she turned to the chicken lot and said, "We're so happy to be getting this eagle."

Happiness, I thought, could depend on whether you're an eagle, or the mayor's wife representing City Zoo. Don turned back to Lucy and drummed his steering wheel. Lucy churped more. He probably didn't buy my exercise bit, and he probably knew the eagle could be grabbed by the ankles and captured, and he probably had the courage to do it. Lucy scratched her head and I remembered I hadn't dusted her. What a way to send her into the world, I thought. The eagle churped again. Mrs. Allison said, "That's darling."

"That's imprinting," whispered in my head, and I wished Lucy would spread her wings and go. The eagle roused and shook. Her feathers had a healthy golden

77

sheen. She stowed her wings and flicked their tips across her rump. Mrs. Allison laughed. "Our eagle flicked its wings like that." When Lucy was settled, Mrs. Allison turned to Krieble. "It would be easier if you turned around and backed our cage up to her."

Krieble nodded and shifted into reverse. Sweat trickled from my armpits and suddenly a breeze came up. Lucy spread her wings. Don paused. Mrs. Allison frowned. I breathed, "Miraculous." The mocker became silent. Lucy's Kruger flaps came out, she opened her primaries and flapped. Don shifted into neutral. The eagle lifted uncertainly. Mrs. Allison's hands wrung, she bit her lip and asked, "Dan, are you sure it can't fly?"

With my spirit soaring, I shook my head. "When I've let her out for exercise, she never has." Mentally I urged Lucy, "Go." The eagle deployed spoilers, dropped back to the roof and retracted her wings. My heart sank and I added, "She likes it here." I was surprised at the drop in my voice.

Lucy slowly extended her wings again. "Fly, Lucy," I whispered.

Mrs. Allison turned to me. "Is it a boy, or a girl?"

"Girl. Lucy."

Mrs. Allison's eyes sparkled and she turned back to the eagle. Don shifted into reverse and started backing. We turned and watched through the truck's rear window. As we rolled, the cage rocked.

We were nearing the lot's corner when two kites circled above the eagle and whistled. Lucy watched them. One folded its wings and dove. The second followed. Lucy glared at the onrushing kite, hunkered and opened her beak as though trying to bare fangs. The truck's bed edged close to the lot's fence. Don stopped, shifted, turned his wheels, and we moved forward a couple of yards. The kite buzzed and zoomed. Lucy turned her head and followed its flight. The second kite flashed in and rapped her a good one on top of her head. Mrs. Allison winced. The kite zoomed and whistled. A feather drifted from its track. Mrs. Allison turned to Don and asked, "Please hurry."

Don shifted into reverse again, looked back and resumed backing. A kite whistled, dove and rapped the eagle's head. The blow knocked her off balance. Mrs. Allison's hands flew to her face. "Oh, no." The second kite started its dive. Lucy spread her wings and moved her head side to side. The kite rapped. Lucy bobbed and shoved off. Mrs. Allison lunged forward and screamed. "Oh, my!"

Don stopped backing. I smiled.

On laboring wings, the eagle dropped rapidly and skimmed above the ground. Undulating tips of the bird's wings brushed the grass. "Oh, my!" Mrs. Allison said again. Out over The Prairie Dog Town Fork of the Red, Lucy ponderously flapped. The kites bombed her in one, two, three series. Doggedly, she lumbered on. Approaching the slanting ground at the cliff's base, she seemed to want to land but was uncertain as to which way to go. The kites regrouped.

The kites one, two, three'd again. Lucy lurched left and fluttered toward the base of the cliff. The kites reformed, did wingovers and slanted down at top speed. Lucy aimed for a clearing between cedars, veered away as if she had changed her mind, aimed at a

79

different clearing, backflapped, reached with her legs for the earth and plopped. Against the cliff's steepness, the eagle landed more on her breast than her feet, and the cliff's slant probably saved her from worse. When she hit, she lurched forward, exposing white under-feathers of her bottom side and legs, reminding me of a can-can dancer's rear view skirt flounce. Mrs. Allison gasped. Lucy gathered herself. The cliff's rise forced the kites to pull up early to avoid crashing against its rocky face. Mrs. Allison glared at me. "Can we drive over there?"

Reluctantly, I nodded. "There's a trail around the waterfall."

She glared at Don. "Hurry, please."

Don stroked his chin, shifted into neutral and shrugged. "That's a pretty wild bird, Mrs. Allison."

I breathed a bit easier.

"Maybe we'd better look for another one for you." The kites maneuvered into new positions and screamed down.

Her eyes blazed. "I want that bird." She looked at Lucy. "I've come a long way for it, and I want it."

A kite roared past Lucy's head, followed by another, and another. Three bunches of feathers drifted. "To where she is, is quite a climb. And she might be hard to catch."

Mrs. Allison kept looking at the eagle. I suspected she was worried about what the town, and the ladies of her club would say if she returned to Iowa empty-handed. The kites reformed and dove. Lucy awkwardly waddled under the outer branches of a cedar. The kites buzzed the bush, whistling as they roared over. Lucy peered through the branches at the birds. Mrs. Allison looked from Don to me and back to Don. "Can't we at least try?" Her voice was high and nervous.

Don narrowed his eyes on Lucy. In a moment he turned to the Iowa mayor's wife. "Let's find you a new eagle."

Mrs. Allison stared through the windshield at Lucy. Tears welled, and she seemed embarrassed. I felt sorry for her. After a moment, Don extended his hand across her to me. We shook, and he said, "I'll be in touch." He shifted into gear. I opened the door and got out. I told Mrs. Allison I was glad to have met her and wished her luck. She sat rigid. I bet her grandfather would have preferred that Lucy was left on the ranch rather than zooed. I closed the door and Don accelerated up the dirt road. The empty cage rumbled.

I took a deep breath and realized how tense I had been. My empathy for Mrs. Allison's disappointment mixed with my exhilaration at Lucy's escape. I turned back to the eagle. The kites buzzed Lucy's bush again. I felt for the eagle too and reminded myself that freedom demands a price for the opportunities it offers. Suddenly I realized Lucy was actually free and a case of the qualms shrouded.

When the eagle was in the chicken lot, I knew where it was. The bird was easy to feed, easy to dust, easy to watch and protected from the canyon's other creatures. Now where was I going to feed her? How was I going to dust her? How was I going to teach her to catch rabbits? How was I going to protect her from Mississippi kites? Don's truck crawled the switchback up the face of Palo Duro Canyon and my qualms deepened.

Lucy stayed under the bush almost an hour before waddling out. In the open, she faced the cliff, leaned into it and started walking uphill. She looked comical, with her primaries crossed over her rump, picking her way between stones on legs and feet poorly designed for walking. She reminded me of an elderly man walking stooped, with hands clasped behind. She had moved only a few feet when a mockingbird flew in and landed. The mocker screeched, sailed down, landed on a rock nearby and seemed to say, "Hey everybody, look at the dumb eagle, walking up the side of a cliff." As Lucy progressed, the mocker hopped to rocks matching her level and screeched more, almost as if laughing. Lucy's presence on the cliff was similar to the arrival of a new kid on the block.

After Lucy climbed about fifty feet she stopped, I supposed to rest. From out of nowhere a sparrow hawk sliced down, zoomed above her head, cackled a high-pitched "killy-killy-killy," turned, dove again and rapped the top of her skull. Feathers trailed the hawk. The little bird had a span of about eighteen inches and weighed no more than five ounces. The eagle watched the bird's zoom. At the top of its rise, the hawk cackled, turned and dove. Lucy glared and opened her beak. The sparrow hawk came on, but pulled out a few inches above the eagle. The hawk cackled past. Lucy waddled under the nearest cedar. The kestrel turned on its tail, dove, flat-hatted the bush, screamed and flew on.

I checked on Lucy every half hour until it was time for me to leave for work. When I drove out, she was still under the cedar. Driving up the switchback I stopped on a turn above her level. Then I remembered that a white patch of feathers about the size of a silver dollar showed on her breast when her crop bulged full, and turned inward and showed less as her crop sank. About twenty-five cents worth of white. I studied the terrain, figuring how I might get food to her. Lucy and her bush were about a fourth of the way up the cliff. To approach her from the bottom seemed logical. It struck me as humorous to consider climbing a cliff to deliver food for a creature with huge wings and speeds up to a hundred-and-seventy-five miles per hour. I made up my mind to find out if eagles are smart enough to come for their food. A roadrunner appeared next to Lucy's bush. The roadrunner swished its tail and gawked. Lucy eyed the bird. I yelled at her, "You're free, girl. Exercise your privilege. Pay no attention to the hawks, the kites, the mockers, the roadrunners. What do they know?" The canyon echoed my voice. She watched the roadrunner. I wanted to stay and see what happened but was out of time. Driving on, I decided to come back to the ranch between my six and ten o'clock broadcasts.

It was near sundown when I approached the rim. The first bats were out from the Indian cave, and a few lightning bugs twinkled. As the sun sank between clouds and horizon, Lucy remained hunkered under the cedar. When darkness came she was still there. Disappointed that she hadn't flown, I went back to work knowing I'd have to check on her early in the morning.

I'm a late stayer-upper and a late riser, one popularly called a night person. After wondering why some of us seem to be day people while others are night persons, I think it possible we might trace our individual proclivity from caveman ancestors. In that era, part of a village's tribesmen no doubt rose early to stalk game active during predawn hours. Tribesmen who remained behind, incidentally protecting women and children, could rest and be fresh to sally forth at sundown and hunt game active in the evening. When morning hunters returned they kept village protection unbroken when evening hunters left. It seems logical that the morning hunters would retire early, and the evening hunters would sleep late. Considering my choice of work hours, I think I descended from night hunters.

Early morning sky was deep blue when I stepped onto my bedroom's stone porch and into July's morning cool. It was the first sunrise I'd seen in months. Lucy was cruising low along the cliff's edge. The eagle's full spanned wings and opened primaries accentuated her size and made her look like a feathered overcast. As soon as she saw me, she turned, hovered and churped. Although her flight was a little unsteady, I imagined Lucy confirming her lift by the sound of air whispering over her wings and around her body. I went back inside for binoculars.

When I came out, Lucy was edging along the ridge to a point straight across from me. She churped again. I raised my glasses. No white showed on her breast. A sparrow hawk, looking like a fly by comparison, cackled into my field of view. The hawk rose up the cliff. Its light underside was difficult to spot against the sky, while the eagle's brown was easy to see. Both bald and golden eagles have dark undersides while nearly all hawks have light undersides. Differences in underside coloration between hawks and eagles may stem from the fact that hawks stoop on game from relatively close range. Selective breeding may favor individuals with a light underside and thus more difficult for prey to see against sky. On the other hand, eagles stoop from a mile or more. That distance coupled with the eagle's high speed apparently provides an element of surprise overshadowing a need for bottom side camouflage. When I'm tramping the wilds, my rule for identifying hawk or eagle is: light breast and/or underwings is a hawk; dark breast and underwings is an eagle. The exception is the black hawk, but that bird has only four-foot wings. The kestrel climbed above Lucy. She eyed the bird. The kestrel rose higher, cackled and dove. Feathers floated again. Lucy landed ungracefully on the cliff's edge and waddled under a cedar. The hawk dove on her bush, dove again, then cackled down the rim as if to say, "When you come out, silly eagle, I'll be back."

To see the king of birds treated with disdain by so many reminded me of the Finn Lauri Rapala. Rapala had noticed that in schools of minnows, hunter fish invariably stalked and attacked those fish with a swimming flaw. Sensing that he could be on to something Mr. Rapala carved a minnow of wood with a limp. The lure was so attractive to game fish that Rapala manufactured his bait and shared his fishing success with fishermen around the world. I also recalled similar experiences with chickens and a cow as a ten-year old in Shawnee, Oklahoma. When one of our chickens wasn't "normal," it was immediately picked on by other chickens. And I'll never forget the first morning I drew the chore of putting a rope on Bossy and taking her to pasture. I was small for my age and leery of the thousand-pound cow, whose horns were untrimmed. To offset possible problems, I tied a rope on the animal three times longer than my father used. When I led her from the lot, she seemed more frisky than when Dad was in command. I played out rope and got as far away from her as I could. Instantly, she started bucking and snorting and acting as if she were going to tear up the world, starting with me. From the way she acted toward me compared with Dad, I'm certain she sensed my unsureness. Rattling in my shoes, I hung on and when her demonstration didn't destroy me she settled down and we went on to pasture.

For life forms to recognize when another isn't up to par seems a natural law. In my view, Lucy's solution to problems with her neighbors lay in her getting her act together. Question was, was an "imprint" capable of getting her act together enough to mingle with other wild creatures? When Lucy had backed her wings and landed so soon, I felt denied of the beauty of the eagle's flight. On my bedroom porch I stood and imagined the continuing problems Lucy would have with neighboring birds. Then I pictured her trying to learn to hunt under a hawk-kite barrage. Harassment would be enough, but hunting to whistles and cackles announcing her whereabouts to big-eared game within a mile seemed the bottom of futility. If she stayed near, no problem. I could take food to her, if I could find her, and if her head feathers outlasted her tormentors. Movement on the cliff near Lucy's bush caught my eye. I raised my binoculars. Five coyotes were coming toward the eagle.

...y, one day old.

...out a week old,
'being fed a
...iece of chicken.

Currie Ranch Headquarters area.

Practicing flying in the chicken lot.

On top of the feed house
the day she flew free.

A red-tailed hawk
Lucy tried to play
'drop the rock" with.

On top of Dan True's VW

After chasing minnows on a hot day. Note wet feather on leg.

Feeding by the waterfall near the Currie Ranch Headquarters.

bout to take the rabbit held by Dan True.

Coming for food.

Lucy's chicks raised
by her in her ninth
nesting season.

•9•

The coyotes moved on long slender legs. The lead coyote was a male. Generally, the father coyote moves ahead of his family, meeting life's risks first. The second was also male, but younger and probably the sole survivor from last year's litter of four or five. Before year's end he would leave the family and establish his own. The next two animals were youngsters, surviving pups from this year's litter. The last coyote was a mature female and probably mother of the family. I have noticed that among predators, which tend to mate for life, males usually lead females and family. Among herd animals, where one male has his herd of females, that male stays behind his harem. Frivolously, I wondered if men who walk beside or ahead of their mates, thus meeting the street's risks first, tend to be more faithful than men who walk behind their wives. For sure, men who walk behind have more opportunity to search the eyes of oncoming females without detection than men who walk beside or in front of a mate. The mocker sailed to a cedar next to the leading coyote and screeched. A second later, a kite dove on the front prairie wolf, screamed and pulled out above the hunter's head. Paying no notice, the coyote moved toward Lucy. When he drew near, the eagle spread her wings, thrust her head, hackled and opened her beak at the animal.

A few feet in front of Lucy, the wolf stopped and studied her through green eyes. Strung out several yards behind him his family paused. The lead coyote sniffed at Lucy. The eagle opened her beak wider. The coyote simply looked. After a moment the wolf sniffed again. Lucy stood still. A moment later the coyote lowered its head, turned and sauntered down the rim away from Lucy. His family followed. The scene reminded me of a Disney film showing an eagle-cougar encounter. The Disney eagle had also spread its wings and hissed, and the lion had also turned and departed. The movie scene caused me to think it possible quadruped predators avoid skirmishes that might risk eyes to eagle talons. In fact, since moving to the ranch I have discovered that foxes, bobcats, and coyotes won't touch dead hawks, owls, or eagles. As the coyote family moved away, they periodically stopped on the rim's edge, turned broadside to Lucy and looked back at her, as though satisfying their curiosity. After they had looked their fill they moved on, although the two youngest invariably stopped after a few steps to look again. Each time, the female waited. Lucy gathered her wings, and the coyotes took their last looks and sauntered out of sight into a draw. The mocker and kite followed the coyotes. The eagle's breast was dark. I was determined not to chase across Texas after her. She'd have to come to me.

By mid-morning it was hot. Even so, Lucy crept from the cedar and flew again, I hoped to hunt. White roundels on her wings and her white-banded tail were prominent. Two kites sailed in and took turns tearing feathers from her head. After the kites' third dive, the eagle landed on the rim and clomped under a cedar.

By late afternoon, Lucy was trying to eat cedar sprigs. Sorry for her, I wondered what an eagle's metabolic conversion rate was for cedar. A moment later she seemed to be trying to eat a tree branch. I felt guilty, but at the same time determined to wait her out. On the other hand, it was possible that the kites and hawks had rapped some sense out of her head. I cupped my hands toward the eagle and told her to hang on, that I'd bring lunch.

There were no rabbits in my fridge. Irritated, I went hunting.

It took until sundown to get a cottontail. As I approached home with it, a sparrow hawk was buzzing a different bush. Another flight,another landing, I mused and parked. Lucy was in the shadows of the bush the hawk was buzzing. She was about a quarter of a mile away and three hundred feet above my level. I carried the rabbit to a weed-grown cement slab, about the size of a big room, a short distance from the bunkhouse, and toward the canyon. Air was still. The hawk quit Lucy's bush and flapped away, I supposed to perch for the night. At the slab's corner, I waved the rabbit back and forth in front of my knees and whistled. "Come on, Lucy baby." She walked from under her bush, faced me, muted, did her head thing, unfurled her wings and sailed off.

With her wings backed into a delta, Lucy flew a track that angled downward. Her head was thrust forward, her legs dangled, and feet and talons were relaxed. Wind tore through her feathers with a whine that convinced me she was hurtling in excess of a hundred. Concerned, I quit waving the rabbit. She roared on and I realized that she could crash into me. I tossed the rabbit on the slab's corner and trotted aside, away from the line of her track. Lucy banked and kept her course locked on me. I trotted faster. The bird banked again and I knew I was the eagle's target. I ran.

The eagle flashed across the cement pad. When she was almost on me, I turned and backpedaled and threw my arms out. At the last second she rotated in front of me, opened her feathers and flapped to break speed. Sticking with me, her wings whooshed air over me while talons jabbed at my face and stomach. Stumbling, I hollered, "No! Lucy, no!"

Talons, wings, and eagle eyes filled my vision. I sidestepped sharply. Lucy was unable to match my turn and plopped on the ground and glared as if to say "Where's my rabbit?" Her wings were poised for launch. I lunged at the cottontail, grabbed it and flung it so that it would tumble in front of her. The eagle grabbed the rabbit, squeezed and glared. My legs were rubbery and my heart throbbed. I backed away and stood rigid. As soon as Lucy "killed" the rabbit, she dragged it into weeds growing in a crack at the cement pad's far end. Wet with sweat I sat down and shook.

I have known people who were afraid of snakes, afraid of storms, afraid of flying, and so forth. "Afraids" have been foreign to me, and although I have been polite toward people's fears, underneath my patience was thin. With my heart pounding and my hands shaking, I realized that I had been afraid. Lucy tore into the rabbit with snaps, crackles, and pops as if nothing had happened. I replayed her talons snapping in front of my face and sat there absorbing this new emotion. I wasn't sure if I wanted to rejoice or mourn the loss of my innocence and wondered why I hadn't known fear before. Lucy swallowed a furry piece. Twilight made the eagle's feathers glow and her eyes sparkled. I laid back on my elbows, crossed my ankles and continued to shake. One thing seemed sure. I didn't care if the eagle ever came back. A rear leg minus its foot disappeared in one gulp.

As the eagle fed, I slowly realized that in a way her lack of fear of me was a compliment to my success at imprinting her, and imprinting had done at least two things: made her unfraid of me, and made her regard me as a walking grocery store with shelves filled with rabbits. In her hunger she probably didn't see me lay the cottontail down and was only snapping at the shelves, trying to find food. Put in another light, she had come at me as a demanding child, as we have seen demanding children "attack" their mother's skirts in a fit for some tidbit miraculously discovered by the tyke at their eye level in a supermarket. The difference between Lucy and a child was that she was equipped with seven-and-a-half-foot wings and vise-grip talons. I reasoned that a wild eagle would fly its demands only at a natural parent. Suddenly I was exhilarated by Lucy's level of imprinting. The power of having an eagle fly to me from a quarter of a mile was heady. But what might she do if for some reason we couldn't get together on feeding for a couple of days. Crazed by hunger, would she charge and possibly hurt a stranger? I pictured how scary it could be to have an eagle snapping at someone who knew nothing about eagles. Maybe stories of eagles attacking people are true, but such eagles were people-raised "tykes" that had become excessively hungry when the people who raised them weren't about at feeding time. Lucy swallowed another rabbit part. "Lucy," I said, "you've got to learn to catch rabbits." Suddenly she reared back and shook her head as though a bone was jammed in her throat. I jumped up and ran for her.

The eagle backed from the rabbit and stretched her neck as if trying to dislodge whatever was bothering. She opened her beak as if to retch, backed again and wiggled her head and neck more. A few seconds later, she turned to the canyon, took a couple of running hops and flew. I stepped to look at the rabbit.

Lucy's rabbit was crawling with big red ants. With my foot I pushed the rabbit aside. It had been lying in a red ant bed in the cement's crack. "Darn," I said and looked across the canyon at her. She had landed about halfway up the cliff and was wriggling her neck. Her breast showed a small amount of white. In gathering darkness the young eagle plodded under a cedar. I hoped the experience hadn't affected her trust.

As I fried chicken for supper, I again replayed my introduction to fear and concluded that throughout my life I had apparently been successful at pinpointing possible fear-producing situations and isolating potential fear in cocoons of knowledge. For example, before I went into crop dusting, I practiced cutting my duster's engine on fake runs. After discovering what the aircraft would and wouldn't do with a dead engine, I wasn't afraid to fly low. But with Lucy I had no advance knowledge on how to deal with a hungry, attacking eagle. As I ate I decided I owed thanks to the bird for forcing me into becoming a more complete person. And in the future, I'd respect other people's fears. Then I remembered that Lucy would be hungry in the morning and that I had no more rabbits. I pushed away from the table, went to the cement pad, sacked what was left of the rabbit and its ants in plastic and stuffed it into the freezer.

Before sunrise I thawed the bunny in my microwave and carried it in its sack to the cement pad. I also took a kitchen chair for protection *a la* lion tamer. With confidence I searched for the young eagle. I found her sitting next to last night's bush. Her crop was sunken and dark. I tossed a pinch of grass into the air to determine wind conditions. The grass drifted north. If she launched, the wind would slow her speed across the ground slightly. If she decided to soar, the cliff would deflect air upward and provide upslope air she could ride like an invisible elevator. She could ride the upslope to hunt, and I debated flashing her with the rabbit, or giving her a chance to move toward independence. Although she was hungry, she probably wasn't on the brink of starvation. I reweighed the risks of waiting for her to get hungry enough to come to me against offering her the rabbit then. I decided that as stepparent in charge of her learning, I should give her an opportunity to stumble onto a rabbit. I put the sack of rabbit under my chair and sat down to watch. A few minutes after sunrise, Lucy muted, did her belly dancer head routine and took to the air. With little food aboard she was light and gained altitude easily. The young eagle turned parallel to the canyon wall and rose on the current.

When Lucy reached the rim she ceased flapping and spread her wings and tail full sail. Lice-damaged notches showed in the tips of primaries in her right wing. Soaring slowly, she followed the rim, using spoilers one wing at a time to drop a wing and make gentle turns along the rim's contour. Her head pointed down, as though she were searching ground below. She seemed eager, but didn't act dangerously hungry. Past the switchback road at a point where the rim turned north, she paused and hovered. Upslope wind would be lost if she turned north with the rim, and her hovering suggested that she was coming to an understanding of that. She let the air carry her up, then cautiously turned back left. It was the first turn reversal I'd seen her make and she seemed to have done it with uncertainty. When her turn was complete, she cruised with increasing skill back along the rim in the morning's gathering light.

Lucy flew past yesterday's refuge cedar and over an old telephone pole with one cross arm. Years ago the pole had supported Currie Ranch's first phone line. The eagle sailed on down again to where the rim turned north. She hovered a shorter time, turned back with greater certainty and flew smoothly to the point beyond the switchback. Hardly hesitating, she turned back and cruised the rim again. Her flying was so graceful that I thought, "If there is reincarnation, I'd like to come back an eagle." As she passed the phone pole, I noticed her breast was without a trace of white. If she didn't catch, and I fed her up there, she might come in more slowly, and more gently. I carried my kitchen chair and sack of rabbit toward my car. As I stepped onto the drive in front of my garage, the sound of an aircraft engine drummed. I stopped and looked back. A red and yellow Super Cub burst over the cliff. The Cub banked toward Lucy. She held her spot in the air, almost as though she were curious. I hollered at her to dive. She held her position. The aircraft closed on her. "Dive, Lucy!"

The eagle hung motionless.

·10·

The Cub banked and returned to its original course.
Only the pilot was aboard and I wasn't sure if it was the
same airplane involved in blasting Lucy's mother. Regardless, I didn't like the pilot's discovery. Lucy watched
the aircraft's image fade, and I now decided that if I
were reincarnated I'd like to bring my brain along.
"Killy-killy-killy" echoed from the cliff and in a flash of
small wings the eagle's skull was rapped. Lucy folded
her wings and landed and got under a cedar and the
hawk went its way. Her total flying time had been no
more than five minutes. Maybe the falconers were right
about the imprinting myth. Maybe Krieble, the eagle,
and I had bitten off more than we could chew. Maybe
the eagle would have been better off in a zoo. Feeling
subdued, I turned for my car to drive to the rim and
feed the young eagle again.

When I splashed through The Prairie Dog Town
Fork of the Red, I was surprised to see the eagle back in
the air. She was diving as if she were after something. I
stopped to watch. Near the ground, she pulled up and
climbed as if gathering height to set up a bombing run.
At about a hundred feet she backed her wings, nosed
over and accelerated toward Texas. Below her a brows-

ing doe deer stopped feeding and trotted a few yards. Lucy leveled and roared up the animal's spine. She stood as much chance to catch the deer as a dog would to catch a car and I saw her deer dives as comical. The doe raised its head and Lucy pulled up. Had the animal been a buck the eagle would have crashed into horns. Chuckling at her innocence, I proceeded to the rim and got out with the rabbit. Low and almost over me the eagle churped and drew in her wings and probably popped her spoilers. I tossed the rabbit into the grass and got back in my car. Lucy landed and ate. As she fed I put my binoculars on her and studied her eyes for ticks. Small sores on her eyelids said her parasite population was getting out of hand. I could catch her with an old Indian trick, but it was an awful lot of trouble. Against the chance that parasites might put her down, I'd keep close tabs on her. One thing was sure, if lice put her down she'd be no trouble to catch, provided I knew when and where. Again I felt subdued.

During the next several days, the eagle learned she could practice flying during predawn minutes before kites and sparrow hawks were out, and during the last few minutes before dark, after the smaller birds had roosted for the night. On her limited schedule, the eagle's total flying time per day was not more than ten to fifteen minutes. An improvement, but not enough. We needed to have the kites leave, to go wherever it is they spend the winter. In *Peterson's Field Guide to the Birds of Texas* I looked up migration habits of Mississippi kites. My handwritten notes on page 57 said I had seen hundreds of the kites forming up over Amarillo's Ross Rodgers Municipal Golf Course on August 24 last year.

I recalled being on the seventh hole. Another notation said the birds were absent from the golf course and Currie Ranch two days later. I presumed that meant they had flown back to Central and South America for the winter on August 26. Chafing at the idea of playing a waiting game, I turned to "Sparrow Hawk."

According to Peterson this little bird was a year 'round Panhandle resident. I considered the veterinarian's idea of blasting the critters from the air with my 12 gauge, but instantly rejected it as a tempting push-button solution that in the long run would fail. Until Lucy handled the problem, there was no solution. She'd have to learn to live with her neighbors without outside interference. Humorously, I thought anyone who believes "eagles kill deer because they dive on them" would be a pushover for "hawks kill eagles." Then one afternoon an approaching thunderstorm emptied the canyon's sky of birds, and Lucy grabbed her chance to fly. She also learned a hard lesson about flying in rain.

With lightning flashing and thunder rolling, Lucy came from under her bush and launched. She flew five minutes before the rains came, but seconds after rain began, she sank behind the rim at a rate of descent that said she didn't go down on purpose. I dashed to the house, got my raincoat and sped up the wet switchback with my windshield wipers on high.

Twenty-five yards back from the rim, Lucy was standing in grass. She was soaking wet, but if she'd made a bad landing, she didn't seem hurt. With her feathers clinging like a wet T-shirt the eagle looked smaller and forlorn. I wanted to take her home, but she was too formidable. I considered putting my raincoat over her, but then I'd get wet and that seemed a bit much. With rain pelting, I told Lucy that she was a big eagle now, and it was time to learn to get out of the rain. She scratched her wet head with a wet claw, and I saw an opportunity to treat her with flea powder. Leaving her sitting in the rain, I hurried home and got my canister of the chemical.

Back on the rim fifteen minutes later, I bulldogged an eagle too saturated to fly, gathered her fighting ankles, wrestled the struggling bird to a patch of wet grass and treated her head. Too many lice and ticks crawled to the surface of her feathers. I gave her body an extra dose and released her. She jumped up, indignantly, I thought, roused and shook. Water flew. When she settled her feathers as best she could I noted her primaries extended across her rump about four inches and had apparently reached full growth. I told her to get up in the sky when it quit raining and flirt for a friend to groom her critters. Wet and woebegone looking, the eagle waddled under a mesquite. I shook my head and told her that at least she was good for filming. I returned to the shelter of my car and watched from there.

As soon as the rain stopped, Lucy waddled to the rim's edge. She peered out across the canyon as if she might be thinking of flying. "Surely not," I thought. The eagle shook, unfurled her damp wings and did. Flapping wildly she dropped below the cliff's edge. I ran to the rim and looked over. A third of the way down she had apparently crash-landed on a narrow ledge. I couldn't tell whether she had been hurt or not. A kite arrived and set up a schedule of bombing runs. Lucy opened her beak to the bird and after the kite had its

105

fun, it left. A few minutes later, a sparrow hawk took its turn and left, and the kite returned and played with the eagle again. Between rounds Lucy preened and dried, and the storm rumbled into the distance. I returned home, changed clothes and checked on her from the front porch. With the sun setting she was still on the shelf.

Near the end of the week, I watched Lucy launch near sundown. After a few minutes soaring, she retracted her wings and sped along the rim faster than I'd ever seen her go. At the point beyond the trail she rose, made the tightest turn I'd seen her make and sped back. Her flight reminded me of crop dusting. Following five or six hot-rod passes along the rim, she set her wings for braking, landed, hardly paused and took off on fully spanned wings. The lice-damaged notches in the tips of her primaries still showed, as they would until she molted over five thousand feathers and grew new ones next year. When she was under way she backed her wings and roared along the rim again. To me, it appeared as if she were bracketing the limits of her aeronautical skills. To catch game on the fly she would need to know her flying limits, and once her aerial skills were up to par, it seemed reasonable to expect hunting should enter her mind.

The evening after Lucy's speed runs she launched again near sundown. I had fed her only a fourth of a cottontail that day so her crop was dark, and her weight light. The evening air seemed especially soft, and fireflies occasionally luminesced. Lucy lifted higher above the rim than I had seen her fly. Her head was pointed down and moving in a way eagles do when searching. After she was up two or three minutes, a sparrow hawk climbed toward her. When it was even with Lucy, it gave its high-pitched "killy-killy-killy." Lucy climbed more, then she stabilized, almost as if she were waiting. The hawk rose above her. The eagle watched the little bird in a way that convinced me she was taking the hawk's measure. The hawk reached an altitude about fifty feet above the eagle. For the first time, Lucy held her position and watched the bird over the top of her wing. The hawk sounded off and dove. When it was near, I thought the eagle started to roll on her side. The hawk roared in, banged Lucy's head and climbed. A feather drifted. The eagle climbed at a rate that seemed to be powered by determination. The hawk's momentum allowed it to outclimb her. Above her again, the hawk hovered and screamed. Lucy climbed. The hawk rose a bit more, folded and sliced toward the eagle. When the hawk was about to rap, Lucy rolled on her back and jabbed her talons at lightning speed at the hawk. Sparrow hawk feathers exploded and the little bird tumbled. Lucy righted and watched the hawk fall. The little bird fell in back of the rim without showing any sign of life.

I felt as I did as a kid at Saturday afternoon movies when the hero galloped to the rescue. I wanted to cheer, but at the same time I was saddened that the eagle's rite of passage had come at the expense of a sparrow hawk. On balance, I was less sad than happy. Feeling that she deserved to be fed, I went to the refrigerator. To keep her appetite sharp, to encourage her to hunt on her own, I got only another quarter of cottontail and drove

107

to the rim. When I opened my car door, a kite whistled. When the kite passed without going after Lucy, I whispered, "Little bird, I think you did a smart thing."

Early next morning Lucy was cruising above the rim at what I considered to be a good hunting altitude. Back and forth she coursed and even wheeled once. Suddenly her wings flashed and she dove toward the prairie and out of sight behind the rim. When she didn't rise into view as soon as I thought she should, I imagined her squeezing a squirming rabbit in her talons. Excited at the prospect of real evidence of deimprinting, I got my cameras and drove up.

When I reached the top, she still had not reappeared in the air. I pictured her eating fresh rabbit and my excitement rose. I walked across a small gully toward where my directional sense said she should be. After a hundred yards or so I spotted Lucy hop-flapping across the ground, as if chasing something. A kite dove. Lucy hop-flapped, pounced, and her eyes followed something that was apparently in the air and low above the ground. A kite zipped over. She jump-flapped again. I zoomed on her and fine-focused. The king of birds was watching a grasshopper. I felt sorry for her. Another kite dove and the eagle clawed a yellow and black grasshopper from the grass. It was difficult for her to hold the insect in her talons while she killed the 'hopper. It was gone in one gulp and she looked around. Her actions reminded me that last fall hundreds of migrating Swainson's hawks had stopped to rest on Currie Ranch. Their dark heads above the grass had dotted land from headquarters to the gate. Immature hawks had hopped through the grass, clawing and eating 'hoppers. Lucy hop-flapped again and it seemed reasonable that grass-hoppers were pretty good training for a young prey bird. Lucy chased an especially large 'hopper and I thought maybe we had a new kind of eagle, a grasshop-per eagle, that Audubon had missed. She looked into my camera, churped and flapped straight for me. I stopped filming and backpedaled. Lucy was gaining. Continuing backward I grabbed a mesquite stick from the ground and scrambled into my car just in time. Be-side the car the eagle glowered. I turned my key and told her to wait right there, I'd get her a rabbit.

All I had in my refrigerator was one small sail 'em. When I returned, Lucy was chasing another grasshop-per. I liked her spunk and took it as sign the eagle didn't want to live an imprinted life. When she saw me she churped and came at my VW. Quickly I got out, held the sail 'em by an edge and threw it as hard as I could. Joe was right. Although the rabbit's aerodynamics weren't as clean as a Frisbee's, it sailed. As soon as the flat rabbit came to earth, Lucy snagged the animal, man-tled and churped. When she was satisfied that the rabbit was dead, she stopped squeezing and fed. A moment later a roadrunner showed up and watched. I snapped several stills, then ran several feet of movie film of the two. As Lucy fed, an idea formed. Would it be possible to accelerate the eagle's march toward independence if I released a live rabbit in front of her? There was a dusty trap in Currie's attic that was made to catch 'em alive. "Why not?" I whispered and reached for my igni-tion key.

Within an hour I had a trap set on the south prairie two miles from headquarters in grass made lush by an ooze from spring water. Rabbit signs were prevalent. I left the trap, and as I approached home Lucy was again in the air. She flew with increased grace and turned with authority. I had a feeling of pride. When I parked and got out, a kite whistled. One of the little gray birds was flapping toward Lucy. I got my camera, aimed and waited.

·11·

The kite missed going the way of the hawk by a mosquito's eyelash. For half an hour Lucy flew and one by one, the canyon's birds were jolted into the reality of her discovery that she was an eagle. Each time a bird dove, she improved her timing. The kites also got smarter and pulled out higher, just enough to be out of talon jab range if she rolled on her back. Lucy countered their early pullouts by sideslipping at precisely the right second and backhanding a diving bird with her wing. This tactic forced the kites to pull out even higher, and soon they were running at her with increasing caution and often they gave up after one sortie. She was able to fly as long as she wanted, but when she did land to rest or preen, rather than hunker under a cedar, she perched on a cross arm on the old telephone pole. The second time she landed there a new pest flew into her life.

The eagle had been in the air over an hour when she swung into the wind and approached the cross arm. With her wings spanned to match upslope lift, she eased above the cross arm's end and touched down softly as a butterfly. After landing she held her wings out a long moment before stowing them. The minute she was settled, a mocker flitted up, landed on the opposite end of the cross arm and screeched. The birds looked at each other. The little one swished its tail, screeched again and hopped to the top of the pole centering the cross arm. Lucy seemed to glare at the mocker. The saucy bird screeched and hopped back to its end of the cross arm. Silently the mocker swished its tail. Lucy preened. Immediately the mocker hopped back to the pole's top. Lucy stared at the mocker. The mocker sat still. Lucy resumed preening. As soon as the eagle's head was turned, the mocker flitted to the eagle, planted its feet squarely in the eagle's back and kicked. The impact slightly rocked Lucy. The mocker flitted to the cross arm's end and screeched. Lucy turned her head to the bird. The mocker screeched and swished. Lucy seemed to glower a moment and resumed preening. Instantly the mocker flitted, planted its feet, kicked again and darted away. Again Lucy glowered. The mocker seemed to understand that the perched eagle was powerless against mockingbird kicks in the back. Lucy kept looking at the bird. After a moment the mocker swished a couple of times and glided back to the rim. Lucy watched the bird land and preened again. If one wanted to claim that mockers kill eagles on the basis of a "back attack," I supposed my film would be a gem. Lucy was zipping her first feather when a sparrow hawk dove. I wound my camera.

Lucy opened her beak at the bird. The hawk flicked to one side and roared by at a respectful distance, zoomed up and flapped on. It struck me that the hawk was exaggerating its flap as it went away. Lucy kept her eyes riveted on the bird until it was some distance. The instant she stopped watching, the hawk reversed course, flashed back at bullet speed and rapped her one before she knew what had happened. The hawk cackled as it pulled up and flapped down the rim. Again I thought its flap was exaggerated, as if it were saying, "I'm leaving, silly eagle, I'm leaving." Lucy kept her eyes glued on the hawk until the bird was so far away it actually had left, whether it realized it or not.

It was an absurdity to see smaller birds continue to pester the eagle. If she knew how to catch her own food, she'd be perching in a loftier area, away from the pests. Lucy looked at me and I had a disturbing thought. Had I become part of her problem? Although she was getting smarter, as long as she was dependent on me, it seemed reasonable to assume that she wouldn't advance toward the top of the pecking order among canyon creatures. I think I was so intent on getting eagle film, I ignored her welfare. I was impeding her progress toward deimprinting and not allowing her to take command of her life. I pondered that. Slowly I carried my camera to the house, packed it in its case, put it at the back of my closet and drove off to check my rabbit trap. I felt better.

My trap held a fully grown cottontail. Happy as a kid with a double-dip chocolate cone, I carried my prize home.

Lucy was sitting on the rim in the shade of a cedar that had become her favorite. I tested the wind and carried the trapped rabbit to an open grassy area about a quarter of a mile south of the Hollywood House. Lucy churped. She didn't know it, but she had been enrolled in Rabbit Grabbing 101, and class was in session. I grabbed the rabbit's hind legs, took it from the trap and held the wriggling bunny aloft. Lucy's head moved. She muted and waggled her tail. I waved the rabbit, whistled and hollered, "Lunchtime, Lucy baby," as if she understood. She shifted, as if preparing to fly. I whistled again and the eagle launched, churping as she flew. I wished I could have told her to be quiet in class when live rabbits were present. She churped and kept coming.

The eagle was approaching at high speed. I put the rabbit on the ground and stepped aside. Deja vu surged and I picked up the trap to use as a shield. The rabbit ran. Still churping Lucy banked to match the rabbit's move. Suddenly the eagle hushed. The rabbit scampered on. Lucy tightened her turn to intercept the rabbit's course, and I whispered, "Good-bye, Mr. Rabbit." Suddenly the animal burst across the grass and waggled its white tail, left. Lucy banked left. With its tail still wagging left, the rabbit zagged right. For a second Lucy held her left bank, as though she were mesmerized by the rabbit's left flicking tail. By the time she reversed her bank to follow the rabbit, her mistake had allowed the bunny to gain a few steps. Just beyond reach the cottontail scampered into deep grass at the base of a small mesquite. Lucy followed, but the chase seemed out of her. She made a pass across the mesquite, turned for me and churped. I raised the trap and held it between us.

Since I was a kid in Ruidoso, New Mexico, I have wondered about that flashy white patch cottontails wear on their rears. With so many predators prizing rabbit for a meal, why would rabbits grow a neon sign? Now that I'd seen an eagle pursue a rabbit I knew about how bunnies turn their sign one way and cut another. I smiled at the rabbit's tail-wagging strategy and again marveled at nature's ways. Lucy drew near. I held the trap at arm's length in front of my face and felt no fear. At the last second, practically on my trap's end, she veered away. The whoosh from her wings washed breakers of air over me. It was the first time I'd been in an eagle's backwash and I felt special. She banked and circled, looking over the top of her wing and churping. Patience, I wanted to tell her.

Over the next few days, we discovered mature rabbits not only have smart tails, they also know to run against the wind when pursued. This tactic cut the eagle's attack speed by exactly the wind's speed, and on days when she chased rabbits into a strong wind, the rabbits were able to pull away from her. After a few times of that Lucy refused to chase tail-twitching, wind smart critters. Although she watched the running animals, she seemed to lack the confidence to go for it. Lucy could overcome the wind's disadvantage by climbing, then diving at high attack speeds that would nullify the rabbit's strategy. But I didn't know how to teach her that. Maybe she needed smaller, slower animals to practice on, animals with less-developed strategies and less-confusing rears. I took my trap up to the ranch dump and baited it with cheese and peanuts for rats. When I returned, Lucy was above the rim. In case she was thinking about hunting, I wouldn't feed her until absolutely necessary.

Within an hour we had a rat. When I drove back, Lucy was sitting on the pole. She watched me thread up the switchback, and I mused on how much easier it would be for both of us if her real parents were available. On top I parked past the cut. Lucy watched me

115

take the cage from my car and walk with it toward the pole. The rat scrambled around in the trap. I jumped down a three-foot layer of rock perpendicular to the rim. In front of the pole and underneath Lucy, I held the cage aloft. She peered down. The rat scurried from one end of the trap to the other. Lucy launched and hovered with her head bent down. I lowered the trap and opened it. The rat scurried onto rocky, thinly grassed ground. I stepped back. Lucy hovered. Aggravated, I said, in parental tones, "Darn it, Lucy, go for it." She didn't move.

The rat stood on its rear legs, sniffed the air and with twitching whiskers looked around. Lucy pulled her wings in and lowered a foot or so. The rat dropped to all fours and scampered between grass clumps at the base of the pole. Lucy extended her wings and twisted her head sidewise to see better. The rat sniffed into the shadow of the pole's backside. Lucy pulled her wings in and drifted lower to the same side of the pole as the rat. Her shadow rippled across the ground. The rat scrambled toward the rock layer in back of the rim. Tentatively, Lucy and her shadow followed. A second later the rodent bounded through a crack in the rocks. I shook my head. "Darn it, Lucy." Disgusted, I carried the trap toward my VW.

In a way, the rat reinforced my feeling about the selective force nature puts on what creature gets caught and what escapes predators. Since the rat was smart enough to escape, his smart genes would be invested in his offspring. On the other hand, if I weren't around to take care of Lucy, she'd either smarten up fast, or nature would let her drop through the cracks and end her "dumb" genes. I looked up at the eagle. Her eyes seemed glued to the rock's crack. Although she lost, considering her circumstances I admitted Lucy deserved special treatment. At my car I turned. She hovered over the rocks. I debated feeding her, but decided against it for then. I thought it was safe enough to reset my trap and wait a little while to see if we could catch another rat pretty quick.

During the afternoon I worked on script to match my final Lucy film. Once in a while I pushed from my typewriter to check on the eagle. Twice she was hovering above rocks where the rat had refuged. Once she landed in front of the crack and peered. I kept working. The canyon's quiet was occasionally broken by a sparrow hawk's "killy-killy-killy," or whistling Mississippi kites, but I pictured Lucy handling all comers. Then it sounded as if the kites and hawks were in my backyard. I went outside to see what was going on.

Lucy was sitting on a Southwestern Public Service Company power pole not far from the chicken lot. The pole's lines hummed with 24,900 volts. I felt weak. If she spread her wings and touched both wires at once she'd go up in a blue flash and a puff of smoke. A kite bombed and knocked her off balance. Her wings came out and the tip of her right wing touched wire. I ran toward her. "Get off that pole, Lucy!" A second kite dove. Running as fast as I could, I waved my arms. "Leave that eagle alone!"

·12·

The kite knocked her off balance again, and again Lucy spread her wings. Her tips were within inches of touching the wires. "No, Lucy," I shouted. Seconds later I was near the pole, I slid to a stop, grabbed a stone and hurled it toward the kites. The missile fell short and I wished for Superman's strength. Lucy peered down, as if saying, "Where's chow?" I shook my head and to God's list of drunks and children selected for special care I added eagles. Kites sailed into diving position and milled. I spun, ran home, snatched the chicken breasts and tore the package open as I ran back. A kite dove and Lucy's wings came out again. Several yards upwind from the pole, at a spot that would minimize her chance of touching wings on wires when she flew, I waved a breast and whistled. She muted, moved her head and pushed off. I laid the meat down, stepped aside and picked up a cedar stick.

Lucy flew straight for the breast, touched down softly and "killed" the chicken piece. Had there been any doubts before about my being part of her problem, there were no more. This eagle had to be weaned. From now on I'd not feed her another dead rabbit, or piece of chicken. From now on, she would get only live game.

If she missed, tough. Sink or swim, fly or fall, letting her get hungry enough to snap on the technique of game-grabbing seemed the most merciful thing I could do.

As the eagle fed, I recalled reading of an eagle-proof pole developed by Morley Nelson in cooperation with an Idaho power company. On the chance that Lucy might use the pole again before she was gone, I trotted home and called Southwestern Public Service Company's line supervisor and explained my problem. The Super said an eagle wouldn't use a low pole on such low ground, that they had discovered the birds use only poles on high ground, because those gave a commanding view of the countryside. He added that eagles land on only about 5 percent of their poles, that the other 95 percent are too low for the birds, and for sure a pole in the canyon just wouldn't be frequented by eagles.

I explained that we were working with a special eagle that had definitely picked a pole down in the canyon and asked if he could eagle proof it anyway. He paused and asked, "This the eagle I've been seeing on that program. What's that program?"

"'True Nature'?"

"That's it."

"Yes."

He asked who I was. I told him, and he said they enjoyed my eagle films, and why was Lucy using such a low pole? I told him it had to do with when she got hungry and wanted my attention. He laughed, said the eagle had me well trained, promised they'd proof the pole next time a crew was working in the neighborhood and that he looked forward to my next program on the eagle. I thanked him but didn't tell him I was indefinitely out of the eagle-filming business.

When I returned to Lucy she was back on the canyon pole's cross arm, cleaning her beak on humming wire. Kites whistled and prepared to dive. The eagle churped at me as if asking about the rest of lunch. I figured that if I let the kites have their way, they'd force Lucy to fly. Their presence confirmed my belief that there is some good in everything. Sorry I had thrown rocks at them, I backpedaled toward home to give them space to do their thing.

It took the kites three passes to push Lucy from the cross arm. When she flew I applauded. As the eagle gathered maneuvering speed, they bombed her again and I felt terrible for even thinking about blasting them out of existence. Her chicken snack bulged about a dime's worth of white feathers. The kites dove once more, reinforcing my contention that what often looks like a quick draw, hip-shot solution may not be. At cruising speed Lucy angled toward the rim, and the kites were respectful. When she turned and lifted up the wall, I smiled at how finely tuned nature's creatures are to the strengths and weaknesses of fellow creatures.

At the rim Lucy faced into the wind. I turned for my car to go and check the trap one last time before showering and going to work. When I started the VW, Lucy was rising rapidly, faster than I'd ever seen before. But with a nearly empty crop she was light. A kite made a pass at the climbing eagle and was backhanded by a flick of the eagle's wing. I shifted into gear. Higher and higher she lofted. I shifted into neutral and watched.

120

Soon she was so high that the kites milled below her, and I supposed that was why she had gone there. But she kept going and was soon a tiny spot of brown against blue Texas sky. The kites descended and resumed their midair locust hunting. Lucy stuck to her climb. Now what is she up to? I wondered. I got my binoculars and stepped from the car.

At three or four thousand feet Lucy leveled. It was the highest I'd seen her. From that altitude she had a commanding view of everything within a fifteen-to twenty-five-mile radius. Other eagles within that radius could see her, too. Lucy's head was moving and my mind's eye could look through hers and scan the canyon, its side canyons and surrounding prairie. I wondered if she were hunting, trying to attract another eagle's attention, or simply drawing a mental map of territory within her vision. Since she wasn't wheeling, I leaned toward attention or mapping.

After she hovered motionless fifteen or twenty minutes, Lucy backed her wings and headed southeast. My arms were growing tired and I was glad she did something. She clipped along at fifty to sixty miles per hour. Her flight was different from the kind I'd seen her make. With my arms very tired I watched her track to the south rim, a mile and a half away. She hadn't flapped once, had lost only about a hundred feet and was in a position to see my rabbit trap, which I suspected she did. Above the south rim she turned right a hundred twenty degrees and flew a course paralleling the rim. After about a mile and a half, she turned right again and tracked back toward me. In a moment she passed directly overhead and only slightly lower than when she left. Sailing on, she approached a point high above the cliff and turned back into the wind. She had flown an equilateral triangle with a four and a half mile perimeter in five to six minutes. It would have taken me two hours to trace her flight over the ground. That put me in my place. But what was her flight's purpose?

As Lucy hovered I guessed she had either tested her cross-country wings or made a silent announcement that she planned to leave home. If leaving was in her head, I was certain that unless she graduated from grasshoppers she'd be back as soon as she got hungry. Lucy pulled in her wings and descended, rather suddenly I thought. When she was down to about five hundred feet another eagle appeared in the edge of my glasses. The second bird was a quarter mile to her left, toward the main part of the canyon. Her descent increased, as though she may have popped spoilers. The new eagle tracked toward Lucy. From its size and color I deduced the bird was a mature male. "This could be interesting," I thought.

The nearer the strange eagle came, the faster Lucy descended. She passed below the rim, down into and across the canyon and landed on the hen house roof. The tercel cautiously followed her track and circled the hen house at about a hundred feet. Lucy cowered. In front of her, the new eagle dove, zoomed, did wingovers and flew the arc of a pendulum that traced the shape of a rocking-chair rocker with its bow slightly below Lucy and high points to her left and right. The male was flying a courtship pattern, and throughout his flight, he

122

churped in high staccato. Lucy's head followed him like a spectator's at a tennis match, but when the strange eagle approached the top of its second rocker, she sailed off the roof, landed beyond the chicken lot and hurried under a cedar. The strange eagle circled the cedar twice, then slowly rose toward the canyon wall. Fifty feet above the rim, the eagle hovered two or three minutes, then reluctantly turned and sailed back in the direction from which it had come. Lucy seemed to peer through the branches after him.

As far as I was concerned, Lucy had failed an impor-tant part of the imprint experiment, and she had forti-fied the myth that imprinted eagles would have nothing to do with their own kind. I was disappointed, almost shattered, at Lucy's reaction to the male. But who was the strange eagle? Could it have been her father? That gave me a rush, then I smiled and murmured, "Been watching too many soap operas." But why couldn't it be? Came from the right direction, had the right feather coloring. No other eagle territory between headquarters and where the bird came from. Odds favored father and I had a warm glow. "Shame she didn't take to him," I thought. "He could have taught her to hunt." That reminded me. She was still hungry. I had just time enough to check my trap once more before leaving for work.

My trap was empty.

After I showered and dressed, Lucy wasn't under the bush. I thought maybe she was hunting and drove up the switchback. When I came through the cut, Lucy hovered not more than thirty feet above. Her crop was pancake flat, and I suspected she expected to be fed. Inching along in first gear, I waved out the window. Lucy dropped so low I heard her churping. Suddenly she was a feathered overcast. Not sure how much lower she'd come, I stopped. She hovered a couple of yards beside my car. Legs and talons flashed down. I brought my arm in. She retracted her legs, hung on upslope beside my window and turned her head to me, rotating her face like a curious cat or dog. She was a pretty eagle. I shifted into gear and moved on. I'd buy a second trap on my way to work. She turned to follow. I accelerated as rapidly as a VW will. When I shifted into second, I glanced in my mirror. Lucy was flapping along behind. I couldn't help smiling.

My speedometer said we were doing thirty-five. Her flap was so easy it said she was loafing along. It was four miles as the eagle flies from headquarters to the gate, and I worried about how far she'd follow. Then I pictured how neat it would look if I cruised up to the gate with an eagle flapping behind. That should impress the neighbors. A jackrabbit flashed in front of me. I turned to see Lucy's reaction.

The eagle banked toward the animal, as though considering pursuit. I came back to the rabbit. It was charging across Texas so fast it should have left a rooster tail of dust. I turned to Lucy again. She was following along behind me. Her reaction to the jack strengthened my thought that she needed a chance on something nearer her level of "un-proficiency."

After about a mile and a half, Lucy pulled up, swung into the wind and landed on an abandoned Currie phone company pole cross arm. With her head twisted around in the loose skin nature gave her for that purpose, she watched me over her back. What an opportunity for her to get an introduction to still hunting, I thought. In my mirror the eagle shrank to a speck. I was glad I hadn't fed her.

Two and a half hours later, I was back on the ranch and within half a mile of the pole where I had last seen Lucy. No speck was on its cross arm. I was as disappointed as a youngster when his dog fails to meet him after school. I searched ahead and drove on.

At the rim Lucy was nowhere in sight. I drove down the switchback, up to the south rim, and set my second trap.

I looked for Lucy until sundown. When it was almost dark, I drove to the rim and walked to a point above her usual perch. She wasn't there. For a long time I stood on the canyon rim and looked out into the gathering gloom. Was it possible she had strayed and found a road-killed rabbit on her own? I hoped so, and that she was stuffed, contented and comfortably perched nearby for the night. As night fell I knew I'd be up early in the morning.

I searched through the morning for the eagle without finding a trace. Driving down from the rim I wondered if I had been severe in not feeding her. Guilt surged, and I speculated on where she might have spent the night. After a while my mind returned to where I last saw her. Had her pole brought into range a rabbit that she caught on her own? I imagined her chasing a rabbit across the ranch and, in her inexperience, crashing into a fence. Then a picture of the Super Cub's gunner flashed and I chilled at thoughts of her lying somewhere out on the prairie, wounded and alone. Suddenly I remembered the high voltage pole and hurried.

There was no sign of her, either on the pole or on the ground under it. Slowly walking away I reviewed her high triangular flight. Had she prematurely gone on her way? Or, had she repeated her flight and along the way gotten together with the male eagle? Feeling brighter I scanned the setting sun's sky. When the sun set I was still scanning. In gathering darkness and with galloping gloom I went to fix supper. During supper I realized that Lucy had never been gone so long. I searched my mind for clues that she had learned to catch and found none. I also felt more guilty than ever about the priority I had put on photographing Lucy, and I wondered what else I had done wrong. I went to bed worried.

I had nightmares about being chased by a pilotless, black Super Cub. I couldn't run because my legs wouldn't move. Vaguely I heard my phone ringing, but tried to run again. The phone kept ringing and I kept trying to run. Suddenly I wakened and groped for the instrument. Dawn's first glow was showing. The caller identified himself as Jimmy Gilbreth and said he worked for the highway department. "Yesterday afternoon I found a big bird in a bar ditch we were working near Pantex. Tried to find you yesterday evening but didn't get an answer."

I sat up. "How big and what color?" Pantex is twenty miles northeast of the ranch.

"Seven-foot wings, at least. Dark brown."

My heart sank.

126

"This bird looks a lot like the one you've been show-ing on television."

"Is it alive?" I held my breath.

"No."

I closed my eyes and asked Gilbreth where he lived.

•13•

Gilbreth said he lived in Panhandle at 1212 Park, and if I hurried he'd wait for me before he went to work. Panhandle was about thirty miles from the ranch. I dressed rapidly and headed out.

If the eagle he found turned out to be Lucy, she had been a long way from home. On the other hand, she could have seen the area from her flight, and could make Pantex in under twenty minutes. In her youthful zest, she may have flown more by impulse than wisdom. Feeling really bad, I roared up the switchback. At the rim cut I felt empty.

Driving toward Panhandle, I pictured Lucy tearing at a road-casualty rabbit while a speeding car bore down on her. I could see her flapping from the rabbit too late. My mind's eye saw her in full color knocked into the bar ditch and life fluttering from her as the car sped on. I gripped the wheel. If she had been eating a road kill, I would blame myself for not feeding her. Again I berated myself for allowing selfishness for eagle film to cloud my responsibility. I felt darker and even more guilty. Why is it so easy to imagine the worst? I searched for a different answer. Young bald eagles resemble goldens. Then I remembered that bald eagles don't come into the Panhandle until October. Some other golden, then. I liked that idea better. If the highway worker's find wasn't Lucy, I vowed that the next time I saw that bird I'd give her all the rabbit and chicken she could eat. I pictured the worst again, bit my lip and rummaged my head for identifying marks. New feathers on her head were probably still a different color. Lice notches in her primaries. I didn't want to think about it anymore.

When I turned onto the 1200 block of Park, an orange Texas Highway pickup was parked halfway down the block. I pulled in behind, got out and stepped to it. Yellow eagle feet stuck out from under a green army fatigue jacket. I vaulted into the truck's bed, kneeled and pulled the jacket away. A young golden eagle lay on its back. Feathers exactly the color of Lucy's were jumbled. Entrails spewed from the bird's abdomen. The bird's head was turned sidewise. One eye was closed and bloody. A tall, slender man of about twenty-five appeared beside the truck. "I'm Jimmy Gilbreth, Dan." We shook and he leaned with his arms on the truck's side. "It was in the ditch. I think it was eating a rabbit from the road and got hit."

I swallowed and lifted the eagle's head. My hands shook and I was embarrassed. Crown feathers were all the same color. I felt like whooping, but it seemed inappropriate. I spread right wing primaries. No lice damage. I shook my head. "It's not Lucy." I turned away, closed my eyes and swallowed.

"Glad to hear it." Jimmy rapped the truck. "Where do you suppose it came from?"

I jumped down. "Probably out of the canyon south of Panhandle. Who's your game warden?"

"I don't know. Why?"

"The carcass should be frozen and turned over to a game official as soon as possible. They'll send it on to the National Eagle Repository in Pocatello, Idaho. From there the bird's feathers will be distributed to Indians who use eagle feathers in religious rites."

"Why don't you take the bird and give it to the warden in Amarillo?"

"Got a trash bag?"

"You bet." Jimmy stepped toward his house.

Driving home with the eagle in my trunk I felt relieved, but the question, "Where is Lucy?" hung over me. My mind repeated its list and my spirits lowered even more.

Several miles out of Panhandle, there was an unusually messy jackrabbit on the road's shoulder. Almost unconsciously I stopped. When I picked the rabbit up it came apart. I laid the two messes next to the bagged carcass.

Driving across the prairie from Currie Ranch's north gate, I scanned the sky and eyed Currie phone company poles as far as I could see. Nearing the canyon I stopped and searched again. Reluctantly I went through the cut and started down the switchback. A kite whistled. I braked to a quick stop and got out. The little bird was alone in the sky.

As I neared the stream crossing, I remembered that I hadn't eaten, but I had no appetite. I had just passed the crocodile warning when on my right, about fifty feet upstream, an eagle was sitting in The Prairie Dog Town

Fork of the Red. I stopped. The eagle looked at me and churped. "Lucy," I whispered. "Lucy." I blinked. She raised her head and peered at the water in front of her. Her feathers glistened and her eyes sparkled. I wiped my eyes. The eagle jumped forward and jabbed her talons into the water. With a lump in my throat, I eased ahead for a closer look.

Lucy was grabbing at minnows. I laughed, wiped my eyes again and laughed again. At least she had the sense to go for things that moved. My hand searched the seat for my camera. I got out. The stream rippled a song. On my left the waterfall roared. I wanted to scold the eagle, but couldn't because it would be arrogant to expect that she'd understand. She looked into the water and jabbed. I chuckled and asked her if she'd seen any crocodiles. I also told her that feathered legs weren't designed for sloshing around in water and she should leave fish catching to her smaller, bare-legged, sharper-taloned cousins, the bald eagle and osprey. Lucy splashed after another minnow. I got one of the rabbit parts and held it for her to see. Lucy churped and scrambled from the water.

I tossed the rabbit across the sand next to her. She pounced and "killed." As she squeezed she hackled and looked at me as if to say, "All mine." I looked her in the eye and told her that Mother Nature manufactures furred animals for golden eagles, and the importance of her remembering that. A black-chinned humming-bird zigzagged down the stream and poised a couple of feet above the eagle. The hummer's iridescence shined, and the eagle and the hummingbird eyed each other. I longed for a camera. With a flash the hummer darted toward a swarm of mosquitoes over the waterfall. Ravenously the eagle tore into the rabbit.

Within seven or eight minutes all that was left of the rabbit was the intestinal part and hind feet. Her consumption caused me to wonder if an eagle ate more when free flying than caged. Lucy cleaned her beak on a rock, sat a moment and jumped on the roof of my VW. She looked around the sky, checking it out. I told her that we now had two traps, and that she must learn to catch running rabbits. She leaned forward, spread seven-and-a-half-foot wings and pushed off. Her feet slipped and she barely cleared the roof's edge. When she held course for the cliff, I guessed she was going to a shady spot to digest. I drove through the water and headed up the trail for home. On the way I decided I was missing important film. I'd allow myself to carry a camera, but put photography second to Lucy's welfare.

At sundown one trap held a gray rat. Since Lucy had been flying free, I noticed that her appetite seemed to peak about every thirty hours. Her unsynchronized schedule led me to think nature has given eagles an irregular appetite to keep game from setting regular hiding times based on eagle flights that run on a predictable timetable. By giving eagles a staggered appetite, Mom Nature seems to have tilted the element of surprise in favor of winged hunters. With Lucy full, I calculated the earliest she would be interested in chasing a rat was around sundown tomorrow. I fed the rat peanut butter and cheese and put it in the garage for safekeeping.

The next day Lucy flew at random times, apparently for fun and practice. Each time her crop was flatter. An hour before time to leave for work, I walked to the cement pad and checked her once more. She was in the air, and I estimated she should be hungry when I came home between broadcasts. Hovering above the cliff Lucy watched me walk to my home. Not wanting to tempt her, I moved inside without pausing. Half an hour later I was showered and dressed for work.

When I pushed the sliding door open to go to my car, Lucy was sitting on the edge of the porch. I hesitated and considered getting a kitchen chair. The eagle studied me as if searching, but she didn't seem threatening. I had mixed feelings about her on my porch. I was flattered by her trust. Obviously we had achieved imprinting depth. But for the imprinting project, and its personal challenge, and for Lucy's fate, I felt pressured to do anything that had a chance of reversing her imprinting. To find her sitting on my front porch said how far we'd not come. It also said how far we had to go. Standing in the door I wanted to tell her I didn't see any rabbits running around the porch. But talking to her had to cease. I said nothing. She looked at me in innocence, and that touched. Silently I stepped out and closed the door. I eased down the steps, passing within three feet of the eagle. When I was standing on the walk our eyes were on the same level. Calmly she sat. I looked for lice in her head feathers and around her eyes. She seemed okay. I wanted to tell her I was going to work, that she should hunt while I was gone, but if she didn't catch anything I'd help her. But I didn't say a word. I backed away. Half expecting her to fly at me, I stepped sideways and kept an eye on her as I went to my car. When I started its engine the eagle was still on the porch. I hoped she wouldn't be there when I returned.

·14·

On my way back home I found a nearly perfect cottontail on the road's shoulder. When I picked it up, I realized I had backed a notch away from the sink-or-swim,
fly-or-fall ultimatum I'd given myself. As I laid the
bunny in the front of my VW, I pledged that it would
be used only if she missed the rat I was saving for her
in the garage.

When I was approaching the rim, I was surprised to
see Lucy flying with another bird, one larger than a kite
but smaller than an eagle. They were hovering near
each other with wingtips no more than five yards apart.
The birds seemed to be eyeing each other. I stopped
and uncapped my binoculars.

The smaller bird was a young red-tailed hawk. The
hawk's wings spanned about four feet, indicating it was
male. His profile was identical to a miniature eagle and
his coloration suggested that he was this year's hatch,
which would make him about the same age as Lucy.
Lucy made a small dip below the hawk's level and rose
back even. The red-tail dipped and rose, and the two
birds' cautious curiosity reminded me of puppies at first
meeting. In unison, eagle and hawk rose slightly,

dipped a little, rose and banked into what looked to be the beginning of a game of chase. It was.

The birds chased each other through dives and zooms. Sometimes the hawk led, sometimes Lucy. When Lucy dove toward the hawk, her bulk made her appear threatening. However, the hawk easily outturned the eagle in sharp pullups. After a few minutes of aerial didos, Lucy dropped to the rim and, on the fly, clawed a tennis ball-sized rock and carried it aloft. With her rock-carrying leg dangling, she rose two or three hundred feet. The hawk wheeled to the eagle's altitude. Lucy edged close to the smaller bird. The hawk eased away a fraction. Lucy maneuvered to stay near the hawk and opened her talons. The rock dropped.

The first time I saw eagles play "drop the rock" was after a Currie Ranch eagle, named Her Majesty, was widowed.* The widow's rock-dropping sequence had coincided with her selection of a new mate. Some male eagles that came into her territory played the game while others didn't, either because they didn't understand, were too young or weren't interested. Either way, one by one Her Majesty rejected nonplayers in favor of one tercel who played her game by diving and catching the dropped rock. They spent the summer together and when nesting time came in February, the female initiated a game of "drop the stick." That game ended when she carried the stick into an old nest. Promptly the male eagle repaired the aerie and the next day their first egg came. Since only male eagles know how to build eagle

*See *A Family of Eagles* by Dan True. Wynwood Press, 1989.

nests, I came to believe that rock dropping was the female's test of a male eagle's cooperation quotient. That is, if a new male grasped the cooperation needed to play drop the rock, it seemed reasonable that the bird might also understand the cooperation necessary to build a nest for her, as well as to take his daily turn at egg brooding. Looking back, I concluded that the female's original rock dropping was employed to separate the men eagles from the boy eagles. The event caused me to reevaluate human male-female courtship. After some thought, I concluded that ladies do some rock dropping too. I suspected many men miss the ladies' game, and that the ladies may or may not allow those men to escape, depending on other variables in a woman's equation for mate selection. After Lucy opened her talon and dropped the rock, the hawk watched it fall and hit the rim. The stone clattered over the cliff and ricocheted down into deepening shadows. Since it would be four to five years before Lucy was ready to mate and nest, I guessed she was trying to recruit an interim grooming partner to keep around until something better came along. If that were her decision, it reminded me of a possible parallel in the human courtship arena. Lucy dove, plucked another rock and rose. I admired her persistence and the spark of independence it implied. Tip to tip with the hawk, she stabilized, paused and opened her talons. Again the red-tail watched the rock drop, hit the rim, bounce a few times down the cliff's face and stop in grass at the base below. Maybe the hawk didn't understand, or maybe the rock was too large for his ability. The two birds eyed each other a

136

moment, then the red-tail sailed down the rim, around the point, and out of sight.

When he was gone Lucy flapped toward me. As she drew near I had an idea. Would she take a rabbit from me if I held it high in my hand, in a variation of her rock game? When she was over me she tilted her head down, retracted her wings a little and descended toward me. She came down slowly, as if she were on an invisible elevator. With one eye I searched for a stick while I kept the other eye on her. There were no sticks nearby. Only rocks. She lowered more. Slowly I stooped and got a rock. When I came back up she was almost on me. She was a feathered overcast. Hair rose on my neck. I pushed the rock up at her and suddenly remembered the first eagle I ever saw. Lucy lowered an inch or two. I pushed the rock at her. I was a fifth grader in the Rocky Mountain village of Ruidoso, New Mexico. Lucy stabilized above me. It had been a fall mountain morning, crisp, with blue sky and air scented by juniper smoke from cabin-heating stoves. Lucy's eyes looked at me with intensity. Without panic I stepped sidewise toward my car. As I moved I kept an eye out for a stick. Lucy moved with me. Classmates and I had been jabbering and giggling, walking the pine-bordered road leading toward Ruidoso's consolidated school. Suddenly a huge brown bird had loomed above the pines ahead of us. The bird was so low we heard the whoosh, Whoosh, WHOOSH of its ponderous wings. A stick appeared. Casually I stooped, got it, held it up at Lucy and kept sidestepping. That school morning when the bird had drawn near us a big eighth grade boy had grabbed my

137

arm, jerked me toward the winged giant and yelled, "Here's breakfast, Mr. Eagle." Lucy extended her wings to almost their full seven and a half feet and turned her head at me. I gripped the stick. She remained just above it, and I kept moving. That morning I was convinced I could be the eagle's breakfast, and I had struggled against the boy. Lucy turned her head side to side, as if to study me. I was near my car. The New Mexico eagle had flown right over us and I had turned and watched it melt into the pines. At that time, relief had washed over me. My hand touched my car. With Lucy still just above me with hunger in her eyes I felt for its door handle, found it and scrambled inside. I sat still a moment before telling the eagle to wait, I'd be right back with a rat. I was relieved to be encased in my car.

The trap in my garage was lying on its side with its ends open. Faint coyote tracks marked dust on the garage's floor around the trap. Win some, lose some. From my kitchen I got new bread and peanut butter and drove to check our second trap. It held nothing. I left them both set. Glad I had found the cottontail, I drove back. From more than a mile away I saw Lucy, still in the air. As I drove toward her my mind returned to the idea of seeing if she would take a rabbit from my hand. If I weighed that rabbit, I could begin tests on how much weight an eagle could carry. That could lead to a probe of the "eagles carry off lambs" and "eagles carry off children" myths. And if I set my camera on a tripod and held the rabbit high, I could trip a shutter cable with my free hand. The project was more than I could resist.

The cottontail I selected weighed two and a half

pounds. By the time I came back up Lucy had moved down the rim half a mile or so. She seemed occupied. I parked, picked a hillock on the rim's edge where up-slope would give her lift and set up my tripod and camera. Lucy eased a little nearer, but seemed to be content with where she was. I adjusted my camera's polarizing filter to make its film record the sky at its maximum blue. My mind pictured an enlarged photo of this great bird with its image frozen against a deep blue sky at the instant she snatched the cottontail from my hand. If this picture worked, it would be the crown jewel of my eagle photographs. Satisfied with the mechanics of the picture I went back to my car for the rabbit.

At my car I pulled a deerskin glove onto my left, rabbit-holding hand. Walking back I hid the rabbit from Lucy. She remained fairly high and still about half a mile.

Standing in place in front of my camera I took its shutter release cable in my right hand. Shaking, I looked toward Lucy, lofted the rabbit and whistled. "Come on, Lucy baby!" Instantly Lucy backed her wings, turned away from the rim, and began a wide circle that would set her up for an approach into the wind. In a few seconds she was out over the prairie about a quarter mile in front of me. She banked into a track that would bring her to me directly into the wind. On line, she leveled her wings, lowered her feet, and slanted into a descent straight at me. Her talons hung loose. As she neared, wind flowing by her feathers harped. I estimated her airspeed at fifty. She hurtled on straight as a bullet for me. Her image was growing rapidly. Suddenly my knees were weak.

·15·

About ten yards out, Lucy was so low her keel nearly skimmed the grass. Her eyes were locked on the rabbit. A second later she zoomed up in front of me and spread her wings and tail fan. Claws raked by inches in front of my face. I closed my eyes and fought an urge to duck. Gritting my teeth, I pressed the camera's shutter release. At the same moment a light touch moved my rabbit hand. I turned and opened my eyes.

Lucy was flying away with the cottontail in both claws close to her body. Her touch had been as soft as angel cake. Sailing on straight wings, the eagle turned and flew down the rim, riding upslope with an ease suggesting she could carry more than two and a half pounds. I felt high as an eagle flies and laid plans to set her up with a jackrabbit. If she could handle that, I'd try a lamb. It was then I realized how close the eagle's talons had slashed in front of my face and eyes. Feeling blessed with beginner's luck, I promised next time to wear a baseball catcher's mask. About a quarter mile away, Lucy landed. Smiling, I gathered my photo equipment and walked toward her.

In the shade of a low mesquite away from the rim, Lucy was feeding. On the prairie to one side of her a roadrunner raised and lowered its topknot, clacked its beak, swished its tail, stepped to within a few feet of the eagle and stared like a nosy neighbor. Lucy ate as if the roadrunner didn't exist. I set up my camera. The chaparral clacked and swished closer to the eagle. I ran a couple of frames. Lucy blinked at the roadrunner and took a new bite. The roadrunner stepped and clacked, circling the eagle and her bush. Occasionally the eagle paused and glared at the chaparral, as if to keep the saucy bird honest.

In five to ten minutes she ate everything but hind feet and the intestinal part. Lucy glanced around and cleaned her beak on the grass. The roadrunner ruffled its feathers and stood as tall as it could. Hardly glancing the chaparral's way, the eagle awkwardly walked to the rim and launched. Her crop bulged, reminding me of the nose wheel protruding from a glider's streamlined form. She tucked her feet up, gracefully banked left, soared around the rim's point the same way the hawk had gone and dropped out of sight. She flew with a determination that seemed to say, "I have a better cliff to perch on." I hoped she'd come back above the rim. When she didn't, my confidence in her breaking her imprint chains rose a notch. I also considered it possible that Lucy had flown with the hawk again. If that were so she might observe the hawk catching wild game, and learn something.

It was two days after I held the cottontail aloft before I saw Lucy again. I was coming home in the evening between broadcasts when I spotted her sitting on the cross arm of the pole two miles from the canyon where I had left her the day she followed my car when I had left for work. I stopped under her and got out. Her crop was flat. "Hi," I said. She peered down, and I imagined how we would look to a stranger who happened on a guy standing under a pole talking to an eagle on the prairie. To keep from intruding on what seemed to be her march toward independence, I debated whether to feed her. I decided my best move was to get back in my car and drive on. If she followed, I'd consider feeding. If she didn't, I'd rejoice. When I shifted into second, Lucy launched and flapped along behind me. I speculated on what the stranger would think at the sight of a seven-and-three-quarter-foot eagle flapping across the prairie behind a beige VW.

In my kitchen I took a black-eared jackrabbit that weighed five pounds from the freezer. I thawed the animal in my microwave, assembled photo equipment and drove back up to the rim. Lucy was waiting. Since giving Lucy the cottontail from my hand, scratching the fleas of life had kept me too occupied to rustle up a catcher's mask. With apprehension, I set up to photograph the same as before, but with the addition of a motor drive to my camera. I had also mounted the rig on a gunstock so that I could aim the instrument from my shoulder, like a rifle. I snuggled the gunstock into my right shoulder, lofted the jackrabbit in my left hand and whistled. She circled for an approach.

When she was skimming the grass in front of me, I held her image in my viewfinder. The second she pulled up I fired negatives at the rate of three pictures per second. The camera's mirror slap and the whirr of its motor rewind made quite a noise. Lucy veered and took a track that would take her to one side of my rabbit. I kept exposing negatives. Passing by she looked into the camera and screamed. At the rim she rose, circled and regrouped fairly high above me. Assuming my photo arrangement had upset her, I detached the camera from its stock, rigged it on a tripod and set it to film, as I had done with the cottontail. I looked up at her and whistled. She backed her wings, banked away, held her turn until she was lined up, leveled and sped at me. My heart pounded.

When Lucy swooped up in front of my face, reflex again forced me to duck. I grinned at my inability to keep from flinching and pressed the shutter's plunger. The instant Lucy took the rabbit I whirled, grabbed the camera, aimed, refocused and snapped. She held the jackrabbit with half-bent legs, as if ready to jettison the animal. Her wings were held in a way that said they were braced and she was straining. Rapidly Lucy sank below the rim. I ran to its edge and peered over.

When I saw the eagle, she was about to crash into the canyon's sloping wall. At the last second, she opened her talons and released her cargo. The rabbit bounced and tumbled down the canyon wall into a heap at the cliff's base. Lucy circled down, landed on the rabbit and killed. Her performance had answered what weight an eagle could not lift. At the same time she had destroyed, for me, the myth that eagles fly away with small children in their claws. As to the eagle-lamb myth, I'd have to find out how much a lamb weighs. I stepped away from the rim, gathered my gear and went home to call the animal husbandry department at Texas A&M in College Station.

The average Texas lamb at birth weighs nine pounds. For me that shattered another myth.

When Lucy finished feeding, she cleaned her beak on a piece of dead cedar and sat a while. Her crop bulged so much I thought she might be too stuffed to fly. Curious as to how much she had eaten, I drove around the waterfall and steered onto a narrow, rough trail between the base of the cliff and the edge of the sixty-foot drop-off to The Prairie Dog Town Fork of the Red. As I approached the eagle she was preening. I stopped even with her. She looked at me. Softly I talked to her. She resumed preening and I got out. She paused. I stood still. In a moment she preened again. Talking gently, I dropped to my knees and crept to a point about six feet from the eagle. Again she stopped preening. Softly I asked her how she liked her heavy rabbit and told her I'd not burden her with that much weight again. The eagle looked at me and preened. I scooched closer and reached for the rabbit's rear foot. Lucy paused. I told her to relax, I was doing research on how much eagles eat. I grasped the foot and pulled the bloody remains. Lucy watched with a look that said she might pounce. Cautiously, I pulled the carcass, scooched back, pulled more and scooched more. When I was six feet away Lucy preened again. I stood, slipped the jackrabbit's remains into a plastic bag and drove home. The remainder of Lucy's jackrabbit weighed two and a half pounds.

It was dark when I drove out to return to KFDA for my ten o'clock broadcast. Near the stream crossing a horned owl flapped in front of me. The owl carried what looked to be a rattlesnake. Since rattlers are most active at night, they and owls are at odds for prairie game. With its silent wings the owl has an edge, and probably is the rattlesnake's most formidable enemy. An owl catching a rattlesnake and breaking the reptile's neck with a quick beak twist was an event I wanted on film, but I hadn't solved the technical problems. Driving on I wondered if eagles ever fly at night.

In preparing a "True Nature," I ran and reran film of Lucy carrying the cottontail and her attempt to carry the jackrabbit. From my crop-dusting experience with heavily loaded aircraft, I estimated the maximum cargo she could fly with probably lay between three-and-a-half and three-and-three-quarter pounds. Factoring out her 10 percent greater feather area, it seemed reasonable to assume that when she molted next year and grew a normal feather set, her maximum carry would probably be reduced to between three and three-and-a-third pounds. I estimated the smaller male eagle's weight-carrying ability would be limited to less than three pounds. On "True Nature" I mentioned Texas A&M's lamb weight information, pointed out that it was nearly double that of a jackrabbit and stated that in my opinion it would be impossible for an eagle to lift a lamb. I also pointed out that in this age of a camera in almost every closet, if eagles carry lambs, someone should be able to film such an event as proof. Anticipating that this might not quiet nonbelievers I offered to pay one hundred dollars to the first person taking movie film of a golden eagle carrying a lamb. A few callers still insisted that they, their parents, grandparents, or neighbors had seen eagles carry off lambs. None accepted my photo offer, and it stands today.

Over the next few days, I noticed Lucy was coming to me less for food. I liked to think that our unsuccessful rat try had spearheaded her learning and vaulted her into a successful catch. That thought was augmented at an afternoon feeding where she smelled of skunk. I had chuckled and guessed she had sure enough learned something about catching game, or at least what not to catch. Since she was coming to me less, it was also possible she had picked up pointers from watching her hawk friend, or even her eagle friend. But when I had to feed her I continued to weigh each rabbit and what she left when she finished. On the average she ate a pound and a quarter per day, or about fifteen percent of her weight. A person weighing a hundred fifty would eat twenty-two-and-a-half pounds of food daily to proportionally match an eagle. When she was especially hungry, Lucy ate as much as, but never more than, two and a half pounds at a feeding. To match that gorge a person would have to consume forty-five pounds. To "eat like a bird" took on new meaning. During this time of information gathering on eagle eating habits, the power company was in the neighborhood and eagle-proofed poles near headquarters. The day after that, on my day off, a high point came in my relationship with the eagle.

It was Saturday, between late afternoon and early evening. It was warm and calm, and I was sitting on Turtle Rock above the stream near the mouth of the Indian cave. I had finished next week's "True Nature" and had come to the rock to enjoy the quiet of daylight's closing moments. My cameras were home, but binoculars lay beside me. I was leaning back, with my hands on rock behind me, and my ankles crossed. On my left, the sun was behind the canyon wall's curve. Shadows were deepening while the disc of a moon that would be full in a couple of days rose above the canyon horizon on my right. I hadn't seen Lucy since yesterday morning when I had fed her a half-grown cottontail. Downstream in the beaver pond a bass occasionally jumped. In the small pond below, frogs intermittently emerged among cattails and reeds, and on the far side an indigo water snake slithered along the water's rocky edge. Above the snake, dragonflies darted after mosquitoes. Near the pond's center a turtle surfaced for air, and a belted kingfisher whizzed by at my level. The bird was almost upon me before it saw me there. At the last second it veered away and chattered on downcanyon, looking back over its wing as if saying a few things. After the kingfisher was gone, a couple of bats fluttered from the Indian cave and across the stream and rose up the canyon wall. Motion on my right caught my attention. I turned. Down the canyon about half a mile Lucy was flapping my way. I put my glasses on her.

Her head was angled down at about thirty degrees and swinging back and forth, sweeping territory ahead and to each side of her track. The eagle was flying along the stream's south bank just above its cut, banking when necessary to follow the stream bank's contour. Her crop feathers were about 50 percent white. With that much showing there was little doubt that she had eaten on her own since I last fed her. I lowered my glasses and froze so as not to alert her to my position. As the eagle neared, I smiled in anticipation of the moment she would find me.

The eagle was about twenty yards away when she spotted me. Her wings flourished, almost in a panic. She backflapped to slow, extended her feet and banked toward the stream. A second later she seemed to relax, spanned her wings and tail and made a tight low circle above me. From the circle, she spiraled down, set up an approach and landed on Turtle Rock, not more than five feet from me. Wake from her wings washed over me. Hair rose on my nape. With her eyes about even with mine the eagle studied me in quizzical innocence. Afraid to breathe, I whispered, "Hi." She seemed to trust me completely. "Where you been?" Her eyes were bright and her feathers had a sheen. I studied the eagle's head. There were no lice or ticks that I could see. Occasionally she glanced at something in the canyon. Her wings were so large, in their stowed position they made her appear to have shoulders. We talked softly about her ability to spread those magic wings and go when and where she wanted, and how she liked the big wide world. After a couple of moments, the eagle stepped to the edge of the rock and flew. Her wings whooshed as they scooped air and she gathered speed. My hair rose again. The huge bird sailed upcanyon and around the bend toward the waterfall. Her circling down and landing beside me highlighted the depth of her imprinting. Yet I sensed the eagle was close to going on her own, that it was possible she could already make it without me. Feeling both sad and glad, my thoughts drifted back and I sat a long time on Turtle Rock. When the curtain of darkness had almost fallen, I got up and walked toward the waterfall to look for her.

Lucy was sitting on a power pole beside the trail from

Currie Headquarters and near to the waterfall. I wondered if she were going to spend the night there. To the soft murmur of the waterfall, I sat down and waited in gathering gloom for darkness.

Forty-five minutes later Lucy was still there. In a canyon bathed with moon and starlight, I walked up under her and talked softly to the eagle. When I finished I walked the dirt, moonlit trail home. I'd check on her once more before I went to bed.

At midnight Lucy was gone. But night takeoffs are easy, for man or bird. It's landing in darkness with no lights that tests. Hoping she made out all right, I walked home. I'd look for her first thing in the morning.

I went to sleep remembering her landing beside me.

·16·

It was mid-morning before I saw Lucy flying the rim. Her bones seemed intact and her feathers were unruffled, but I'll never know if she spent the whole night aloft, lucked into a landing somewhere or performed a skillful moonlit return to earth. Rigging an eagle with a tracking radio and following it at night would give us answers. Until then I tend to believe she has moonlight vision and made a night landing. Lucy flew over the rim cut and to the point where weeks ago she learned to make a turn. This time, however, she went beyond. It was the first time I'd seen her go that far west. Concerned, I raised my binoculars.

The eagle continued westward. As she progressed, the canyon shallowed, its edges rounded, and her image shrank. When she was a speck about four miles away, I wondered how far she intended to go, or if her young mind even had an intent. Lucy kept going until she was so far she merged with earth's shimmering heat waves and disappeared. I lowered my glasses and frowned. Eagles normally claim a territory of about ten square miles, roughly the land within a radius of between a mile and three-quarters and two miles from Currie Headquarters. I was surprised she had gone so far. But

Lucy was young and had not established territorial roots. I worried anyway.

At the end of the fourth day, I admitted she might have left home. I worried about her eating and imagined troubles she could get into, including an encounter with the Super Cub. On the other hand, I rediscovered golf and regained precision on ILS approaches at Amarillo International. At an evening dinner party with friends I hadn't socialized with since Lucy, I took a lot of good-natured ribbing for having spent so much time "Walden Ponding" it. But visiting with, and meeting new friends while discovering the delight of mushrooms sauteed in peanut oil and teriyaki brought me back to civilization pleasantly. As I got reacquainted, it was comforting to find I had friends left in the world of humans. I also realized there is more to life than chasing birds and bees.

During the time of my resurfacing, Krieble called and reported that they had found Mrs. Allison another eagle. I asked if he had any idea as to why she was so insistent on having Lucy, that her persistence had struck me as strange. He said he didn't know, but shared my curiosity. I dismissed it as one of those things I'd never have an answer to. Krieble added he was glad Mrs. Allison didn't get "our" bird. I felt he would like to have said more about Lucy's escape but may have been constrained by his official position. I brought him up to date on Lucy. He thought her landing on the rock beside me was incredible. We agreed our imprinting job was done, and the next five years would tell if she could overcome imprinting, take a mate and become a genuine female eagle. He closed with "For now, let's not worry over things about which we can do nothing more." I agreed.

Five weeks after Lucy had gone, hundreds of Mississippi kites formed up in a milling, restless flock over Ross Rodgers Municipal Golf Course. When I played a couple of days later, they were gone. Kites were also absent from Currie and I presumed the birds that bugged Lucy had been part of the golf course flock. Daylight hours shortened, mornings on the ranch cooled, and a few yellow leaves twinkled in the cottonwoods. Then, in the sixth week, Lucy flew back into my life. Her reappearance was unique.

I was in the den, working at my typewriter near the windows. During a pause to think, I noticed an irregular form on the platform of the vine-covered windmill. Deep in thought, I merely noted that a form was there and kept working. In a moment I paused again. Unconsciously my eyes went back to the form. This time I got my binoculars.

The form looked like a golden eagle lying on its breast. "Lucy" whispered in my head, but I had never seen her on that or any other windmill. "Impossible," I breathed and fine-focused. It was a golden eagle. I stepped outside to my front yard. With difficulty the eagle stood. It was the size of a female. "Lucy?" No white showed on the eagle's breast.

The bird shifted on its feet, and something seemed wrong with one leg. The bird faced me. Hair rose on my nape. "Lucy?" The eagle shifted again. One leg was definitely not right. I hurried inside, got a chicken breast and trotted to the windmill.

The eagle watched me approach. I moved down the trail, past the mill, and upwind. At a distance that would give an eagle a comfortable gliding ratio to the ground I turned and waved the chicken. "Lucy?" The eagle limped around the platform's edge to face the wind. She focused on the chicken, moved her head side to side, and took off. I placed the chicken on the ground and stepped aside.

When the eagle landed on the chicken, one leg collapsed and she lost her balance. She put her wings out for support. The eagle's wings had lice damage in the right places. Half lying down, Lucy tore into the chicken. Goosebumps popped all over me. I hurried for more chicken.

Lucy downed five chicken breasts. As near as I could tell her leg wasn't broken, but she didn't use it to hold food, and she toppled when she stood on it. I guessed that in her inexperience she had caught something she couldn't handle, and it had bitten her. A fox maybe, or coyote, bobcat, or raccoon. On the other hand, she may have been shot. When she finished eating she limped up the trail back to the windmill and lay down under it in the grass. I thought about catching her and taking her to the vet but decided for the time being to check on her frequently. If she got worse, I'd take her to town. "If you can catch her," an inner voice said.

Once an hour I checked on Lucy. She seemed contented, and my coming near didn't seem to bother her. Just before sundown she limped from under the windmill and flew down into the horseshoe basin. I lost sight of her when she dropped below the basin's edge, but

153

from the way she flew I didn't think she had gone far. I trotted down the road to the waterfall and looked for her.

The eagle was lying on a narrow sandstone shelf under an overhang a hundred yards from the waterfall and about halfway down the basin's wall. The shelf was snug and protected. I sat down. In evening cool I speculated again on how she may have been hurt. Crashing into a fence in the excitement of chasing a rabbit was a possibility. Or she may have pulled her doe "attack" on a buck and crashed into horns. A kingfisher flew above the stream from the waterfall, diverted toward the eagle and made a noisy fly-by. To know that Lucy came to me for help, as a child in need comes to a parent, was exhilarating. At the same time I realized her six weeks "out" meant she was wild and free. Although it would take four to five years to know if imprinting had twisted Lucy's ability to take a mate and breed, her ingenuity at leaving her world and returning to ours gave me a rush. When darkness came I walked home. I was glad she was back. Just knowing where she was comforted me. For advice on how to handle her injury, I'd call a vet in the morning.

At sunrise I walked to the waterfall with a chicken breast. Lucy was on the shelf. I waved the morsel. Bright-eyed and alert, she looked at me but made no move. A sparrow hawk flew into the basin and circled near her as if trying to figure a way to bug her. After two circles, a respectful distance from the overhang, the little bird flew on. A moment later a wren flitted to the shelf, studied the eagle and flew. I walked home to make breakfast and call the vet.

When I described Lucy's behavior, the vet said he'd like to X-ray and examine that leg. "But under the circumstances, just watch her and let me know if she looks worse." He paused, "You say you hadn't seen her in six weeks, and now she comes back to you for food?"

"Yes. Isn't that neat?" I bubbled.

"Sounds to me like she's an opportunist. Knows a good thing when she sees it." He chuckled.

I thought differently.

Lucy's routine for recuperation became lying on the east canyon shelf in morning's shade and around noon, flying to a shelf on the basin's west side for afternoon shade. It pained me to see her land on her hurt leg, but she managed, and I gave her credit for having sense enough to know if it was usable. To keep her from having to make more landings than necessary, I recorded the time and weight of her meals. With that I was able to anticipate her hunger and take food to her before she might fly for my attention. At first I climbed down into the basin and tossed food up on her shelf. After the fifth day, she began flying to me when she saw me coming. That day she used her leg more easily. From then on she improved rapidly.

The eleventh morning after Lucy's return was clear and cool with a Texas sky that matched its reputation. After Lucy fed on a half-mashed cottontail, she flapped up on a sunny rock next to the stream. Her landing barely favored her leg. She cleaned her beak on the rock, then turned to face the stream. After a moment of looking up and down the canyon, she preened. I eased to a rock within ten feet of her.

Lucy preened a long time, working wing and tail

feathers with care. The sun gave her feathers a sheen and sparkled her eyes. New crown feathers were still a shade dark but bleaching was bringing them to a match. From the overall condition of her head feathers, I assumed she had a grooming partner. I hoped he wasn't distant. When she finished preening, she roused, shook, settled, and flicked her primaries across her rump two or three times. After sitting a moment she lifted her feet awkwardly and turned a little on the rock. She faced precisely into the wind drift and toward the waterfall. A moment later she flew. From the way she flapped I had a premonition she was leaving.

Pumping her wings, Lucy gathered speed. Above the stream she aimed toward the fall. Nearing the fall she climbed, skimmed its lip, and banked for the rim. Not looking back she flapped her great brown wings in graceful, undulating rhythm, but with seeming determination. At the cliff's base she turned parallel to the face of the north wall, full spanned, and rose on upslope to the rim. At the rim she turned into the wind and climbed. She was magnificent. At about two hundred feet she banked away and turned downcanyon. A moment later she was gone.

Near sundown I searched the basin's rock shelves, the windmill platform, and the perches on the north cliff she used early in her life. There was no sign of the eagle. When I didn't see her the following day, or the next, I guessed she had returned to wherever she had already spent six weeks. I was fairly sure I'd see her sometime in the future, but I missed her. Wherever she was I hoped she would tell other eagles she was treated well by humans.

Early in November the red-tailed hawks left Palo Duro Canyon, probably for Mexico, Central America, or Panama. Oregon juncos, or snowbirds, arrived from Canada and Alaska and robins came by the thousands to the canyon's protection from a winter on the prairie. Late in the month the vultures formed up and left in large flocks for their wintering grounds near Mexico City. Then, in November's last week, I was driving on the prairie between headquarters and the gate when I saw two eagles, a male and a female. The birds were in the air above the canyon on my right about a mile away. I stopped. They were playing "drop the rock." I turned and drove across the prairie toward them.

As I neared, the male bird eased away from the female. I kept going, and so did he. The female sank lower. Slowly I rolled ahead. The male eagle went on until he was a speck about a mile away. The female held still in the air as though waiting for me. I eased ahead. When I was almost under her, I stopped and looked closely. The eagle was Lucy.

Ahead of me there was a grassy point of ground. Shallow, juniper-studded draws opening into the canyon were on each side. I got out of my car and walked onto the point under Lucy. She hovered above me. I laughed and waved my arms and hollered up to her. Lucy drew in her wings and flew into the draw on my right. I looked down on the top of her wings. She sailed a few yards ahead to a spot in the air directly in front of me and looked back over the top of her wings. A second later she slipped left and let the wind drift her back even with me. From there she rose a little and drifted toward me. Low above me she hovered again and looked down as if to say, "It's great up here. Why haven't you learned to fly?" She flew her pattern around me again, hovered briefly, then spread her wings and rose. As she climbed she angled toward the male eagle. Her wings whispered music in the sky. Wild and free she sailed on. I watched her a long moment before turning for my car. I walked with a warm glow.

EPILOGUE

That first winter, I often went into the canyon below Currie Headquarters to check on Lucy. Nearly every time, she would fly to me and hover low. Her male companion invariably stood off a mile in the distance. I guessed that at some point in his life he had been shot at and either narrowly missed or wounded. I wished she could have told him I wouldn't harm him. Regardless, his shyness toward me underscored her innocence. For Lucy's future protection against trigger happy hunters she might fly near, I considered altering her trust in humans by firing rifle or shotgun blasts to one side of her. Although my logical side pressed for me to do that soon, my emotional side sidestepped the issue by promising "sometime."

The two birds occupied the territory of Lucy's birth. (In the eagle's society, widowed females remain in a territory and attract a new mate, whereas a widower male will leave in search of a domain held by a female. Lucy's father had probably followed that social contract.) After Lucy had hovered above me awhile she'd usually circle once or twice and return to her friend. He stayed so far away I couldn't determine his age, but it seemed unimportant. Occasionally I saw them hunting together, she with her larger size flying low to scare game from the bushes, he with his smaller, zippier size hovering above and behind, poised to dive and catch. As in nest building, whichever bird is best suited for a task performs that task. From a survival view that makes sense. It also brings to mind that nature's directing of tasks to a male or female by suitability is operative between male and female lions. The smaller, less powerful lady lion is the hunter and provider in a lion family. Can you imagine the hunting chances of a male lion belly-stalking a gazelle through grass too short to hide his massive head and that flashy mane? Every gazelle within sight would chuckle, trot out of the way, and a lion family would go hungry. Differences in lion-hunting assignments, and male-female eagle-hunting assignments reconfirm my thought there is a reason for everything in nature. At the same time, I wonder if there aren't lessons there for our man-woman joint efforts.

An amusing event happened before Lucy went on her own, which I couldn't find an appropriate spot for in the body of the story. It was a fall afternoon. I was giving Guyon and Mary Francis Saunders from Amarillo a tour of the ranch when we saw Lucy trying to entice a young sparrow hawk (wing span about eighteen inches) into a game of "drop the rock" with a stone that probably weighed four times the hawk. When the eagle carried her rock aloft, the hawk watched with interest, but made no effort to dive when the rock was dropped. After about three drops, the sparrow hawk went its way, leaving Lucy hanging.

Near the end of that first winter, KFDA's news department covered a story involving a red-and-yellow Super Cub that crashed on a Panhandle ranch and killed the two men aboard. Investigators found a 12-gauge automatic shotgun in the wreckage.

When Lucy was a year old she molted and lost her lice-damaged feathers. Her new wing feathers were without the white roundels on their bottom sides, and the white band across her tail fan was narrower. Overall, her brown was a shade lighter, and although I no longer had a positive way to identify her, when a two-year-old female eagle flew to me within Lucy's portion of Palo Duro Canyon, there was little doubt in my mind as to who the eagle was. She was so unafraid I considered again firing a gunblast near her, but still didn't have the heart.

Since releasing Lucy, I have discovered that when I release imprinted hawks brought to me by Krieble or other game officials, the birds quickly learn the ropes of wild living from kindred birds, in the same way kids learn from those down the street. With hawks, including red-tails, it was simply a matter of setting them free. These birds easily survived on grasshoppers through their learning period. Eagles, on the other hand, needed a ready source of easy food to see them through their learning time. I don't think this means hawks are smarter than eagles. I think it's more a case of food quantity needed to keep an eagle going. To survive on grasshoppers, the bird would probably need a yard wide mouth and a cruising speed of at least a hundred and fifty.

After Lucy's fourth molt, she was brown overall, with a brush of tan at the carpal joint on the top of her wings (about halfway out) and a brush of tan in her tail feathers. In the February of her fifth year, which marked the fifth anniversary of when her mother laid the egg she hatched from, Lucy and the male played an aerial game of "drop the stick." After a few midair catches between them, she flew the stick across the canyon and landed on an old nest site within a hundred yards of the nest where she began life. The male followed her and repaired the aerie she had chosen. Two days later I walked to a point above her nest. She looked at me as if to say, "Oh, it's just you" and stayed on her nest. Softly I asked her to fly and let me see how many eggs she had. She simply sat. I raised my voice, and she still sat, looking at me unconcernedly. To make her fly I was forced to dangle a rope over the cliff and across her beak. She had two eggs and hatched both. The second chick, however was killed by the first within a week in what is known as the Cain-Abel battle.*

When Lucy was six I moved from the ranch. When she was thirteen I revisited in March and found her on a nest with two eggs. She simply sat and looked while I talked to her from ten yards away with a *PM Magazine* camera crew (Tom Moore and Carla Aragon) from Albuquerque's KOB-TV looking over my shoulder. Her mate had lost none of his shyness and stood off a mile or more orbiting high above the canyon. To make Lucy fly again required a dangled rope. When she flew, she circled back over us and hovered. Ecstatic as a kid at finding a long lost treasure, I hollered and waved. She stayed above us long enough to convince me she ex-

*See *A Family of Eagles* by Dan True. Wynwood Press, 1989.

pected a rabbit. I was glad I had never made her afraid of humans. Her nest held two eggs that produced a male and a female. There was no Cain-Abel battle and the boy eagle fledged in June. The girl fledged in July.

Lucy's territory within Currie Ranch is isolated enough from the rest of Texas to protect her from outside threats. She could survive decades, and for the interest of her eventual fate she should be banded. At some point in the future, I probably will catch her and perform that task.

When Lucy comes to me and hovers, it still chills and probably always will. That she recognizes me after so many years suggests that imprinting apparently made her a crossover. Environment furnished the eagle access to our civilized world, while heredity equipped her for life in the wild one. Lucy is a regal, universal eagle. I feel privileged that we are able to share her life.

* * *

The year Lucy would have been twenty years old I returned to Amarillo. Twenty is a healthy middle age for an eagle, and if Lucy had survived she'd have mated and been assimilated into her life as it should have been.

Exploring the canyon, once again, within what had been Lucy's territory, I spotted an eagle's nest, with a bird sitting it. Could this eagle be Lucy? A strange bird would fly away at my approach, but the "rabbit test" would be the real determinant. Would this eagle let me approach and offer a rabbit?

Rabbit in hand, I walked cautiously toward the nest. I could see the male eagle circling; he was having no part of this intruder. But the sitting bird sat motionless. I heard myself crooning the same nonsense sounds I'd made so long ago to the baby Lucy, heard my voice with its flow of soothing patter. She let me approach nearer than I'd ever been to an eagle in the wild. She took the rabbit from my hand! The bird was Lucy! She hadn't forgotten me.

For the next three months, I watched and photographed—Lucy, her mate, their two youngsters. Observing them all at incredible closeness, I was overwhelmed again and again by their beauty and nobility. The majestic continuity of their being, which in some small way they permitted me to share, brought back so many memories of the joy of our time together.

Another chapter in Lucy's life is again another story, one I hope to draw together in the not-too-distant future. It will be my privilege to share again with my readers but a small slice of the heritage, the drama, the grandeur of our American wildlife.